Praise for *You Can't Touch My Hair*

"Phoebe Robinson has a way of casually, candidly rough-housing with tough topics like race and sex and gender that makes you feel a little safer and a lot less alone. If something as wise and funny as You Can't Touch My Hair exists in the world, we can't all be doomed. Phoebe is my hero and this book is my wife."

—Lindy West
New York Times bestselling author of *Shrill*

"*You Can't Touch My Hair* is the book we need right now. Robinson makes us think about race and feminism in new ways, thanks to her whip-smart comedy and expert use of a pop-culture reference. The future is very bright because Robinson and her book are in it."

—Jill Soloway, creator of *Transparent*

"*You Can't Touch My Hair* is one of the funniest books about race, dating, and Michael Fassbender. The world is burning, and Phoebe Robinson is the literary feminist savior we've been looking for."

—Hasan Minhaj
senior correspondent on *The Daily Show*

"Phoebe Robinson says the things that need to be said, and does so eloquently and hilariously."

—Mara Wilson, author of *Where Am I Now?*

"Moving, poignant, witty, and funny... A promising debut by a talented, genuinely funny writer."

You Can't Touch My Hair:
And Other Things I Still Have to Explain

Phoebe Robinson

JACARANDA

This edition first published in Great Britain 2022
Jacaranda Books Art Music Ltd
27 Old Gloucester Street,
London WC1N 3AX
www.jacarandabooksartmusic.co.uk

Published by arrangement with Plume, an imprint of Penguin
Publishing Group, a division of Penguin Random House LLC

Photo credits: pp. 28, 32, and 185: courtesy of the author; p. 49:
photo by Michael Ochs Archives (Getty Images); p. 50: photo by
CBS Photo Archive (Getty Images); p. 53: photo by Ian Showell
(Getty Images); p. 56: photo by Paul Taggart/ Bloomberg (Getty
Images); p. 57: photo by John D. Kisch/Separate Cinema Archive
(Getty Images); p. 59: photo by Ebet Roberts (Getty Images);
p. 60: photo by Ron Galella, Ltd. (Getty Images); p. 61: photo by
Rocky Widner (Getty Images); p. 63: photo by Tim Mosenfelder
(Getty Images); p. 66: photo by Rob Kim (Getty Images).

Plume is a registered trademark and its colophon is a trademark
of Penguin Random House LLC

A CIP catalogue record for this book is available from the British
Library

ISBN: 9781913090999
eISBN: 9781914344008

Cover Design: Rachel Willey
Cover photograph: © Mindy Tucker
Typeset by: Kamillah Brandes
Printed and bound in Great Britain by Clays Ltd, Elcograf S.p.A.

MIX
Paper from
responsible sources
FSC
www.fsc.org   FSC® C018072

More by Phoebe Robinson:

Everything's Trash But It's Okay

Please Don't Sit On My Bed in Your Outside Clothes

Contents

For my parents, Phillip and Octavia. I love you.

Forword

Work wife (*n*): That person at your job (same or opposite sex) that takes the place of your "at home" spouse while you are at work (this is not a sexual relationship). You talk with, connect to, and relate to this person as good as or better than you do your "at home" spouse with regard to all things work-related.

(Source: www.UrbanDictionary.com)

Phoebe Robinson is my work wife. We've been official for about two years now, ever since we met on a field piece I was shooting for *The Daily Show*, which led to us starting our live show and podcast, *2 Dope Queens*. Even though our careers keep us busy, I am happy to report that our relationship is still going strong. Phoebe still texts me pictures of Bono about once a week and asks me if I would "smash" him. (My answer is still "Fuck no, never in a million years.") She still refers to me as either her Oprah or her Gayle depending on what kind of day we are having. She still tells terrible dudes at bars that insist on having shitty conversations with us to

Please buzz off. I'm in my thirties. She always says, *My eggs are dying. I don't have time to hang out with anybody that I don't want to.* Fair enough. And even though Phoebe is only thirty-one, and I am twenty-six, she still insists on giving me the most weathered advice possible, as if she has seen some shit. Advice like: "Doggy style is a great position to have sex in, that way you can have a little bit of *you* time. You can get some work done, you can think about your taxes or about what groceries you need to get tomorrow..." She somehow manages to say this with all the wisdom and strength of Cicely Tyson. That's Phoebe, though.

When I first met Phoebe, she introduced herself to me, but she didn't even have to—I had already known about her because she was a black lady involved with Upright Citizens Brigade who, like me, also mostly dated white dudes. I could blame my previous knowledge of her on the fact that UCB is a small community, but I ain't gotta lie to kick it. I had low-key stalked her before meeting her that day. Anyway, she didn't pick up any red flags from me, so she invited me to co-host her monthly live show, *Blaria*, at UCB. Our first show together was like a great first date. I found out onstage that night that Phoebe was able to vocalize things that were deeply important to me. That being a black woman *and* a feminist is a full-time job. Like, #fuckthepatriarchy even though we both usually date white dudes who look vitamin D deficient and probably burn in the sun too easily. That black lives do matter. And that we both think that Carrie Bradshaw was a fucking stupid idiot for breaking up with Aiden for Mr. Big. Like, really? The man is a carpenter; he could literally make her furniture. And he even bought the apartment next door to hers so he could combine the two. The man wanted to *MacGyver* her living space! I think I can speak on behalf of all straight women everywhere when I say, "Hi, hello! Sign me up for that, please!" Clearly, Phoebe and I were bonding at a rapid pace, and after the show, I knew that being friends with and performing with Phoebe Robinson was good for my soul and I wanted to continue to do that as much as I could. This is how our podcast *2 Dope Queens* was born.

Phoebe's ability to talk about the importance of bell hooks as well as her dreams of hooking up with Colin Firth are a part of what makes her so wonderful. She is a badass black feminist and somehow manages to stay #woke while not taking herself too seriously. She is delightfully petty in that way that leaves us giggling and talking shit about everyone around us when we go out for drinks. And she is brilliant onstage. Even with all the comedy shows that we have done together, Phoebe still manages to surprise me and make me laugh until I pee myself a little bit by accident. She is one of my best friends, and I am so excited that you bought this book and are about to spend time with one of my favorite people on this frequently shitty little miserable planet that we call Earth.

Last New Year's Eve, my boyfriend and I did shrooms and talked about the lovely texture of the couch while we watched the ball drop in Times Square on TV. After the countdown, I asked my boyfriend what his New Year's resolution was. He said, "I think it's to be more like Phoebe." So I thought about all of Phoebe's qualities for a second—her brilliance, her strong values, her beauty, her humor, and her strength. All of those things are what makes Phoebe wonderful. Not only is she my work wife, she's my shero. "Hell yeah," I said. "I want to be more like Phoebe, too."

—*Jessica Williams*

Introduction

The other day, I was thinking about the first time someone of a different race gave me a lady boner. It was more than seventeen years ago—February 24, 1999, to be exact—and I was watching the GRAMMYs. Let me give you a little bit of background about myself during this time. I was a fourteen-year-old movie nerd and an "everything school-related" slacker. I'd often refer to myself as a "tomboy," until I learned that liking and watching sports but not actually being *good* at them does not make you a tomboy, it makes you a human. So, yes, I was a fourteen-year-old sports and movie lovin' person/nerd who thought that watching award shows was the bomb.tumblr.com, probably because I'd never won anything. So seeing people at the height of their artistic achievements was the ultimate fantasyland for me: I cried along with Hilary Swank as she graciously accepted a best actress Oscar for her performance in *Boys Don't Cry*. I pretended I was up there with Lauryn Hill when she did a touching and intimate rendition of "To Zion" right before snagging a

GRAMMY for Album of the Year. And I laughed when Italian actor Roberto Benigni ('memba him?), who was so overjoyed at winning the Oscar for Best Foreign Language Film that he walked on the backs of people's seats to get to the stage. Award shows gave me hope that maybe I would also do something equally impressive with my life, that I could have a future outside of Cleveland, Ohio. Nothing against the Cleve, but I just had a feeling something cool outside those city limits awaited me. Watching these awards shows was my way of preparing for my future successes, I told myself, and was way more interesting than, say, studying for chemistry class. And in my eyes, there was truly no greater award show than the 1999 GRAMMYs. During this golden age of pop culture achievements, Hill was the belle of the ball, Madonna was killing it in her "*Ray of Light*, earth mother phase," and Will Smith won Best Rap Solo Performance for "Gettin' Jiggy wit It."

I know. Looking back on it now, it's kind of ridic.edu that out of all the songs nominated, including Hill's "Lost Ones" and Jay Z's "Hard Knock Life (Ghetto Anthem)," that Smith won Best Rap Solo Performance. But the '90s were full of bad choices, OK? Like guys in boy bands wearing golf visors when they weren't golfing, the movie *Battlefield Earth*, Lou Bega and his "Mambo No. 5" bullshit, pizza bagels, the Gulf War, Utah Jazz point guard John Stockton wearing short shorts on the basketball court, and me spending three weeks trying to memorize the lyrics to Barenaked Ladies' "One Week"—after those twenty-one days, all I got down was: "Chickity China, the Chinese chicken." Three weeks, guys! That's all I got! The point is, in the '90s, mistakes were made. Lessons were learned. And thanks to Ricky Martin's "The Cup of Life" performance at the 1999 GRAMMYs, I learned that my vajeen is capable of quaking over non-black dudes the way the glass of water did in *Jurassic Park* when dinosaurs were nearby.

Martin may now be considered a slightly cheesy performer whose music is only played as a throwback jam at a wedding or bar mitzvah, but think back to '99. Martin was gorgeous, he sang with passion and swag, and he commanded the stage like he knew this set was going to be his breakout moment into the English-speaking music market. He was so *dreamy*. And it didn't hurt that he could work those hips. Simply put, I was stunned. I was in love, but I was also surprised—I was never really drawn to a non-black guy like this before. Not that I was ever anti-non-black dudes; they just never really were on my radar because they didn't look like me. And I think that most folks would agree with me when I say that it's human nature to be drawn to people who look like us, especially when we're younger and not very exposed to the world. So that first time I felt attracted to someone outside of my race, it felt, for a moment... transcendental. As in, I, Phoebe Lynn Robinson, had transcended past race! That I was capable of seeing *people* and not their skin color. In other words: I was (drumroll, please) *postracial*. Yeah… No.

Look, dude and lady boners can do a lot. They help create babies, embarrass their owners for appearing at inopportune times, and make people overlook flaws in others—such as having a boring personality or being a DJ—because the boner is too busy giving a thumbs-up to an attractive person the way the Terminator does at the end of *T2* when he is drowning in hot lava. But existing as a signal of postracial living? Nice try, but no. Sexually desiring someone who does not share your skin tone is not some grand sign that society is becoming postracial, no matter what anyone tells you. The truth is, people *love* throwing the term *postracial* around. Americans are *so anxious* to move on from the sins of our forefathers that we're on the lookout for any and every symbol that our national nightmare of racism is over. And finding someone who has a different complexion than us hot is a quick way of saying, "See? We did it! Racism solved!" But sexual attraction is just the tip (*heh*) of the iceberg. It seems like we've been looking for our "get out of jail free, we're postracial" pass for quite some time.

Even though the term *postracial* is everywhere these days, it's actually been part of our lexicon for a while. It was first used in a 1971 *New York Times* article titled "Compact Set Up for 'Post-Racial' South," which claimed that the topic of race was going to be usurped by concerns of population increase, industrial development, and economic fluctuations. Ever since then, *postracial* has been marched out fairly regularly anytime something positive happens for POCs (aka people of color). Taiwanese-American basketball player Jeremy Lin being an NBA star? Postracial! Mexican cooks at a Jamaican jerk-chicken restaurant? Postracial! My bestie Jess (who you met in the foreword) and I being upgraded to the front row at a Billy Joel concert just because?* Postracial! A white makeup artist rubbing my legs down with lotion to prevent me from getting ashy. She knows what ashy is?!?!** Postracial! You get the picture. And to many, there is no greater symbol that the postracial era is upon us as when Barack Obama was elected president of the United States. No matter where you stand politically, there's no denying that in 2008, we were coming off the heels of a presidency that left the country disillusioned thanks to 9/11, the war in Afghanistan, and Hurricane Katrina. So when Obama appeared on the national scene with a message of hope, change, and "yes, we can!" much of the country happily got sucked into this tornado of positivity, and it seemed like anything—like a postracial society— was possible. I totally understand the reasoning behind this line of thinking. His election is certainly historical,

---

*   Apparently, Billy—he and I are on a first-name basis, BTdubs— doesn't like coming out and seeing a bunch of *American Psycho*–looking mofos chilling in the front row with their arms crossed at his concerts. So he has his staff look for women that he would find beautiful and put them in the front row. Is this very #YesAllWomen? Probably not. Is it pretty much the reparations Sojourner Truth envisioned? I'd like to think so.

**   Actually, *this* is reparations, and if I were the queen of a country, this would be the salutation white people would have to greet me with.

and along with it came a sense of hope and change. But as a nation, we are far from the "everyone holding hands in racial harmony" that we assumed would happen once Obama was ushered into office. In fact, throughout the Obama years, there has been, at the very best, resistance to change, and at the very worst, a palpable regression in the way the country views and handles—or more accurately, *refuses* to handle—race.

We only have to turn on the nightly news to witness the significant uptick in police brutality toward black men and women. Eric Garner. Trayvon Martin. Sandra Bland. Laquan McDonald. Rekia Boyd. Yvette Smith. Shereese Francis. Timothy Russell. Malissa Williams. Sean Bell. Oscar Grant. Miriam Carey. And that's just the tip of the iceberg. MappingPolice Violence.org states 37 percent of unarmed people killed by police last year were black, even though blacks only make up 13 percent of the US population. And these types of deaths are happening with such frequency that it's almost impossible to keep track of each individual case and mourn the loss of life before another victim appears. Oof. Unfortunately, this is not just an American problem. This sort of police brutality is a worldwide phenomenon. Additionally, the UK's *The Guardian* newspaper published research from the Equality and Human Rights Commission (EHRC) stating that "police forces are up to 28 times more likely to use stop-and-search powers against black people than white people and may be breaking the law" to do so.

While these incidents are devastating, the average person experiences racism in lesser life-threatening ways. Microaggressions, or slights/snubs/insults, that reinforce marginalization of a particular group are the more common way that racism manifests on a daily basis. Normally, my run-ins with racism come in the form of jokes that I "talk white" or that I'm not like "*other* black people," as if that is some sort of compliment. Other times, I may find out that I have lost out on a job in entertainment because they wanted a white woman instead. All of those are, unfortunately, standard-issue, and while they are upsetting in the moment, I tend to use that mixture of anger and sadness to propel me forward. I would have run out of tears a *loooong* time ago if I let every time someone was racist toward me devastate me. Still, even though I'm fairly used to micro-aggressions, there are those occasional situations that manage to surprise me, and not the "I found a $20 bill in a winter-coat pocket" good type of surprise. I'm talking like the "Aunt Flo decided to visit when I just put on a brand-new pair of my Victoria's Secret five-for-$25" type of bad surprise, as was the case with my recent Uber ride.

To properly set the scene, you must know two things: One, I had just finished working out at the gym and decided to treat myself to a cab ride home. Yes, this is trifling, but when you're so single that your Apple TV remote has its own side of the bed, you really try to do anything to make yourself feel special, hence the Uber; and two, my driver looked like Villain #4 from the Taken movies, you know, just real Slavic AF, so for the purposes of this story, he will be known as Taken Face. OK, now to the story.

During the drive home, Taken Face got into a fight with a belligerent white driver and yelled, "Fuck you, nigga," while Bill Withers's "Lovely Day" played in the background, which, as a friend later told me, "if this were a romantic comedy directed by Spike Lee, this would be your meet-cute*." Unfortunately, this wasn't a movie, but real life. And in real life, there's always that awkward moment when a white person realizes they just said the N-word in the presence of a black person, so the white person makes the same face that Dustin Hoffman made in *Rain Man* when he was assessing how many tooth-picks were on the ground. Taken Face quickly came to the conclusion that *literally anything* would have been better than saying a racial slur to the other driver. So next comes the apology, right? Wrong. Instead, Taken Face tried to make amends with me by showing me pictures of his

---

*   For those not up to speed, a meet-cute is when two characters who are destined to be together, but don't know it yet, first get acquainted and something romantic/adorably embarrassing that pits the lovers against each other happens. Like Matthew McConaughey saving Jennifer Lopez when her high heel gets stuck in a sewer grate in *The Wedding Planner*, or when Billy Crystal and Meg Ryan grow to hate each other, in a charming way of course, as they drive cross-country in *When Harry Met Sally*. Or in my case, Taken Face and I would eventually get past this N-bomb hiccup and fall in love because he'd buy me a Russian winter hat and I'd teach him how to make potato salad for the family cookout.

barely brown daughter. L to the O to the L. Clearly, Taken Face was doing this as if to say, "We're cool about what I just said because she's brown... and you're brown." Nope.com. Let me just say this right now, in case there's any confusion in 2016: If you're a white person and you have references on standby to verify that you're allowed to say the *N*-word, you are probably the *last* person on planet Earth who should be saying *nigga*. Your overpreparedness is very suspicious, and makes you the Tracy Flick of racism. How about instead you use those type A powers for good and teach the world something useful, like how to fold a fitted sheet properly?

In all seriousness, incidents like these happen so regularly that it's impossible to believe that the racism of the past simply disappeared the moment Obama was elected. So what do we do? Perhaps the first logical step is to retire the term *postracial America*. Because much like the '90s New York Knicks basketball team that was never quite good enough to win the big kahuna, but had a lot of heart, the concept of "postracial America" is an also-ran that tried its damnedest to succeed. Obama is not a deus ex machina–type figure whose mere presence righted all our nation's wrongs. The truth is, evolution is slow, glacial even, and it cannot occur without people doing difficult and painful work. That doesn't sound like a whole heck of a lot of fun, which is precisely why it hasn't happened yet. But there's an even harder truth to accept: The kind of growth required to move past race is nearly impossible to achieve because racism is rooted in the foundation of America. (Ahem, the Three-Fifths Compromise of our Constitution, anyone?) Without awareness or acknowledgment of how these things have left a permanent stain on our country, no amount of blind hope is going to remedy the erosion that racism has done to this country. It is something that, until then, people like bell hooks and Ta-Nehisi Coates, and yes, people like me, will fight to explain.

Believe me, it's not something I necessarily *want* to do. I don't wake up every day going, "Aaah! Time to break down institutional racism to people before Kathie Lee and Hoda drink their body weight in Franzia and host the fourth hour of the *TODAY* show." Honestly, I would be just fine spending my time finally perfecting the dance breakdown from Janet Jackson's "If" music video or finally taking an art history course just for funsies or, you know, enjoying the luxury of being a multilayered person like white dudes are allowed to be, but that's just not how things are.

So because I, like many of my friends and family, am on the receiving end of racism, and I, unlike many of my friends and family, have a platform—stand-up comedy and writing—it only makes sense to use it to effect some positive change when it comes to racism, and eventually, one day be right alongside Kathie Lee and Hoda, day drunk out of my mind and ordering sensible cardigans from Net-a-Porter.

But don't worry. Even though I discuss race fairly regularly, I'm not always operating in "after-school special" mode. Sometimes I'm given some hope that we are coming together as a people. Sometimes that hope comes in the form of a friend/ally who defends me after seeing that I'm being bombarded with racist comments on Facebook. Other times, that hope reveals itself in far less noble instances. Like the time when I was crashing on the couch of a dear friend in LA, who happens to be white, and a piece of my weave fell out and her dog started to *eat* it, which forced her fiancé to chase the dog around the living room and wrestle the weave from its mouth, and they were *totally chill* about it, like this happens to them all the time. Hmm, maybe *that*'s a sign that we're getting closer to living in a postracial society.

While we wait to see if that the dog-eating-weave moment will end up in history books, I'm using this waiting period as my chance to pull a Clarissa and explain it all. Well, not *all*. Just three things—my takes on race, gender, and pop culture—because I'm all about keeping things nice and tight, like the jeans in *The Sisterhood of the Traveling Pants*. (Seriously, the four actresses in that movie had different body types, yet the jeans still fit Blake Lively like a glove? How is that possible?) Moving on. I think it's time we get started, but before we get into my thoughts on interracial dating (two thumbs up), lady presidents (two *empty* DivaCups up; not risking spillage over here, folks), and Spotify posting notifications to my Facebook wall and letting my friends know that I'm listening to Spice Girls' *Greatest Hits* album (two middle fingers up like Beyoncé in the "Formation" video), let's start with a fun Q&A so you can get to know this book and its author a little bit better.

One more thing before I start answering your questions. Thank you for buying this book, even though it's not Black History Month Eve! (That's not a real holiday, but it should be. Get Hallmark on the horn, please.) I'm thrilled you recognize that this book is a year-round thing, like deleting your parents' long-ass voice mails without listening to them, or white people wearing shorts. OK, you may begin:

How do you spell your name?

This may seem like a silly question to those who are thinking, *Uh, just look at the cover, dummy.* Never mind those haters! This is an excellent question because when it comes to my name, things like logic and sensibility don't often come into play. Usually, the person will quickly glance at my license or other official document bearing my name, say, "Got it," the way I do when a Verizon representative rattles off my sixteen-digit confirmation number even though all I managed to jot down was the letter *Z*, and then hand me something like this:

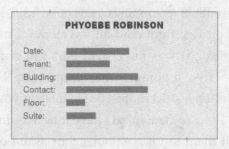

I don't know what happened either, y'all, but it done happened. What was once the name of a character from the TV show *Friends* has now morphed into the name of a new medicine for restless-leg syndrome.

This is all to say that my name is spelled *P-H-O-E-B-E*, and you'll probably forget that in five minutes, but I love you anyway.

And your last name? Kidding! Phoebe, you wrote a book. Why?

You know, I could totally take that "why" as "Hey, crazy lady, why did you write something? There's no way it can measure up to the work of Junot Diaz, Tina Fey, or Shakespeare," but instead I'm imagining you meant "why" in a "Charlie Rose interviewing a celebrity" kind of way, which is "Let's talk about all the ways you are amazing." Thanks for that, lovely reader, and to answer your question, I wrote this book because of all that sweet, sweet cash unknown first-time authors who had a three-line speaking part on *Broad City* get.

You got paid a lot for this?

If by "a lot" you mean $50 and a month's worth

13

of salads with five toppings *maximum* from Hale and Hearty, then yes, I got paid all the money. I'm kidding about the $50; it was more than that. I'm not kidding about the five toppings– maximum rule; Hale and Hearty are some strict mofos. But to answer your "why" question, I'm a comedian, so I have tons of opinions and like to tell them to folks whether they asked or not. So after G-chatting my thoughts about race and gender to one person at a time for several years, I figured why not put everything in a book so people can read them/use the book as a coaster.

Thanks. I just have to say, your hair looks pretty cool.

That's not a question, but tha—

Can I touch it?

And *thereeee* it is. Nope. You can't touch my hair. Even if my hair catches on fire, do not come to my rescue; just let me do a Michael Jackson spin move to put the blaze out. Honestly, there is nothing I hate more than people groping and marveling in *National Geographic*–esque hushed tones about how my hair feels different than they expected. It's frustrating how something as simple as a quick trip to the supermarket can turn into an impromptu seminar about the history of black hair, during which I'm supposed to clarify where I stand in the #TeamNatural vs. #TeamRelaxer debate, discuss how I think black/white relations are going in America, and admit that if I was less defensive about my hair being touched, racism might be solved in an hour.

Uh-oh. There's that R-word again. Is this one of those books that's going to make me feel bad about being white?

No. However, I'm going to touch on some heavy and complicated race issues that might make things a little awkward between us for a minute, like when a daughter-in-law finally masters her passive-aggressive mother-in-law's signature dish, and the mother-in-law says, "It's good... but a little light on the paprika, no?" But I promise we can survive that level of discomfort.

Well, what is this book about, then?

Well, like I wrote earlier, there are tons of things I still have to explain about being a black lady in this day and age. Such as what it's like to be *the* black friend (Hint: It's annoying), what it's like to be black in general (Hint: It's very cool and awesome and also annoying), feminism (See: What it's like to be black in general), and working on-camera as a black lady (none of the clothes fit, and I audition for lots of characters named Laura and Abby, but then lose the parts to actual white ladies named Laura and Abby). Basically all the stuff that makes some dude on the Internet call me a "See You Next Tuesday" is what I'll be discussing here.

Back up. Seems like there's a lot of black stuff going on here. But, from some Internet stalking, it seems that your last two boyfriends have been white, you read Nora Ephron books when you're getting your hair did at the salon, and U2 is your favorite band, so...

Hmm, that wasn't really a question as much as

it was an accusation: "You can't be talking all this 'blackity black black, *blahbity blah blah*' stuff when you go home every night to some CW-looking dude." One, my previous white boyfriends have mostly been AMC cute, thank you very much. Two, reading Nora Ephron while a Jamaican lady braids my hair is pretty much the America Martin Luther King Jr. dreamed of. And three, sure, I may enjoy what some call "white people stuff," like U2, but that doesn't negate the fact that I'm black, which means that when I go shopping, clerks follow me around their store so much that my family crest motto ought to be Rockwell's "Somebody's Watching Me." So I don't care how much dad rock I listen to or how many basic Chris Pine– looking dudes I date, I'm black and I have the receipts to prove it. Literally, I keep all my receipts in order to prove that I'm not stealing from whatever store I walk out of.

I don't know. It seems like this book is going to get deep. Will you judge me for wanting to take a nap instead of dealing with race and feminism?

Not at all! I mean, I have taken a nap during a pregnancyscare because I was like, "Eh, it can wait."

And?

My fallopian tubes got all Gandalf-y and said, "You shall not pass," and shut it down. See? If you had taken a nap, you would've missed that completely medically sound and killer pop-culture reference. There are tons of those in this book!

16

You're going to write about pop culture, too? Probably should've opened with that.

Fair point. I'll remember that for my next book. As for *this* book, there will be lots of stuff about the '90s (Hello, *Felicity* and *Moesha*!), why my niece should use Lisa Bonet and fictional character Olivia Pope as her life guides, and all the amazing moments in black-hair history (I'm looking at you, Angela Davis), and of course, there will definitely be several sentences mentioning actor Michael Fassbender, who's so gorgeous that the mere sight of him will make any straight woman hum "Taps" as she flushes all her birth control down the toilet.

OK, this book sounds somewhat more fun. And you seem fun, too! Can I tell people I have a black friend now?

Wait, seriously?

I'm sorry. You're right. That was inappropriate. To make it up to you, I'm going to postpone my Bones *marathon until tomorrow so I can read this book.*

Postponing a binge-watch session to read this book is probably the nicest thing anyone has ever done for me. And my mom turned her vajayjay into a Six Flags Water Park slide so I could enter the world. Sorry, Mom, but you've just been demoted to number two on my list of awesome people.

I feel we've gotten pretty tight over these last few minutes. What if you close your eyes while I touch your hair? And if it still bothers you, I can give you a cookie, too.

Hmm, interesting. What kind?

Oatmeal raisin?

What I'm feeling right now must be what Freddie Prinze Jr. felt when he was saddled with making over Rachael Leigh Cook in *She's All That*. Screw discussing racism and touching my hair—I now know the biggest challenge of my life: teaching you what a goddamn cookie is.

Sorry about snapping at you just then. It's just that oatmeal-raisin cookies aren't cookies! Ugh, I blame health nuts for perpetuating that fantasy! But enough about that. Time to wrap up this Q&A, which was equal parts fun and informative, like a Pap smear! Hey, did you know that if you get a Pap smear while Kings of Leon plays in the examining room, it's basically like you're having sex. And sex is fun! Anyway, I feel like we covered some of the basics of what this book and I are all about, so why don't you settle in and get to reading my opinions on everything else, while I go talk to my parents about how I know sex is fun. Mom, Dad, come back! I can explain...

From Little Rock Nine to Nappy Hair, Don't Care in Eighteen and a Half-ish Years

Have you ever been milling about your apartment when a TV-MA rating flashes across your TV screen, so you do a Jackie Joyner-Kersee–esque hurdle over the back of your couch because you know some salacious things are about to go down? (No? Just me?) Well, I'm about to drop my own disclaimer, so get ready:

BOOK–OH SHIT Rating: for HEY, WHITE PEOPLE, HARSH TRUTHS ABOUT BLACK HAIR ARE ABOUT TO BE DROPPED.

Sorry. There's no sex, drugs, or violence to be had here. Just a lot of real, open, and honest talk about black hair, and by "black hair," I don't mean the raven color Amy Lee of Evanescence fame sported. I mean African-American hair, and the African-American people who have it. Black hair seems to raise a lot of non-black people's blood pressure. I've seen the gamut of emotion on people's faces—awe, confusion, stress, anger, joy, amazement, suspicion, envy, attraction, you name it—because we, and I'm using the royal *we*, as in

19

society, have never figured out how to have a healthy, functional relationship with black hair. Black hair has always been somewhat mysterious, like who the heck Keyser Söze is or why Forever 21's adult-sized leggings are so small they could double as condoms for sea turtles. And when something is mysterious, people fear it. Fear the Afro, for he who wears it is going to start a revolution! Fear the dreadlocks, for she who wears them must be a drug dealer! Fear the kinky twists, for he who wears them must be an unstable vagrant! And so on and so on. And when you add mystery plus fear together, it equals various forms of oppression, such as how black women who don't have their hair relaxed (aka chemically straightened) have been told they are "unprofessional," or how schools have told young black children they can't wear their hair natural because it's a "distraction" for everyone in the classroom, or the daily, unwanted commentary, such as this unsolicited message I received when I had dreads: "You know, you would be so pretty if your hair was straight." Wow—"hire-ability," acceptance, and attractiveness are all on the line when someone wears his or her hair naturally? That's a lot of weight to assign to a physical attribute.

The fear of black hair has been an ever-present part of America's social history. The tumultuous relationship between black hair and America can best be explained this way: If black hair is the hardwood floor in a Broadway theater, then America is Savion Glover just soft-shoeing all over the floor during a production of *Bring in 'Da Noise, Bring in 'Da Funk*. Outside of skin color, nappy hair is probably the biggest in-your-face reminder of blackness, of Otherness. And in case you haven't noticed, people have historically not handled "Otherness" well. If you don't believe me, then, by all means, dog-ear this page and go do a Google search, or watch *West Side Story*, or save yourself the time and read my supertruncated yet extremely accurate breakdown of the history of the world:

> *"Hey! You don't look/think/act like me, and as Hall & Oates sang, 'I can't go for that, no, no can do.' Stabby, stabby, gunfire, explosion like from a Jason Bourne movie. Yes, I did just quote a lyric from a Hall & Oates song. Who doesn't like Hall & Oates, the face of blue-eyed soul? Oh, you don't? Stabby, stabby, gunfire, explosion like from a Jason Bourne movie, everybody dies." Repeat until the end of time.*

Minus mentions of Napoleon, Tesla, and the invention of peanut butter, that sums up the history of the world fairly accurately, no?

While black hair is no longer typically met with stabby, stabby, gunfire (thank goodness), it still does mostly receive a collective (and not-so-friendly) Dikembe Mutombo finger wag from society. The message that society sends to black women is that their hair does not belong to them but is fair game to be discussed, mocked, judged, used, and abused, and it serves as a home for people's preconceived notions about blackness, as if it is an abstract concept that is not connected to living, breathing, and feeling human beings.

To me, the concern over the state of black hair is so ingrained in society, so ingrained in black people's DNA that it, in some ways, defines who we, I'm using the black *we* here, are to people and subsequently to ourselves. Kind of like how there is Career Girl Barbie, Aerobics Instructor Barbie, and Army Medic Barbie, there is Professional Black Hair (straight like uncooked linguine), Makes-Her-Own-Incense Black Hair (dreadlocks or twists), and Super-into-Malcolm-X Black Hair (Afros, duh), just to name a few. The point is that we are aware that how our hair is styled determines how we will be treated by others, and that treatment or mistreatment (for example, the word *angry* doesn't get hurled at me nearly as much when my hair is straight as when it's in an Afro) can affect our own opinions of ourselves. But this isn't always the case. Some black people haven't been lucky enough to be exposed to differing outside perspectives of black hair and as a result the loudest perspective—the one that says black hair = bad—is often what reigns supreme in their minds. We black girls are conditioned from a young age to treat our natural hair as a problem that needs to be remedied, that we need to have that "good hair," meaning hair that, in its natural state, is not difficult to comb through. I don't know about other black ladies, but my natural hair is so tightly coiled, it gets hella vagina dentata on comb teeth. I. Break. Them. All. The. Time. By societal standards, my hair is The Beast from *The Sandlot*. It's a problem to be handled.

And so I have joined a community of black women throughout history that have embarked on this mission to get desirable hair: undergoing the various hair modification processes (hot combs, blowouts, weaves, and perms/relaxers) that are often uncomfortable and/or painful and pricey, clearing a minimum of four hours from your schedule to get it done, hanging out in a hair salon that has a damn Etsy shop within it where they sell homemade shea butters and baked cookies, realizing that picking out colored weave in the hair store is a lot like going to Lowe's and picking out paint swatches. Compare and squint, compare and squint, compare and squint. And on and on. If you're a non-black lady, you're probably thinking, *That's an* awful *lot of time to be spending on one's hair*. You are correct, but I will say that it's not all just expensive and time-consuming. Black hair is fun! When I have dreads, I feel like a badass Marvel comic superhero. When I shaved my head a decade ago and was bald, I felt free. I didn't have any hair to think about. Yippee!! And when I recently switched up my kinky curls for a beach wave, ombré look, aka the #LowBudgetCiara, I always felt like someone was following me around with an industrial wind fan. Clearly, it's not all just an inconvenient time suck for me when it comes to my hair, and that's also true for other black women. There's an element of play, like being a pop star who constantly reinvents her look. There's also a bond, a band of sisters, if you will, because when we see each other, we know *exactly* what it took to get our hair to look a certain kind of way. In a simple look, a whole conversation can happen, which often boils down to "Queen recognizes Queen." In a glance, we can recognize our sister, dap it up, do the Kid 'n Play dance, let her know that we know what she's going through and more. With black hair, there's a whole culture of shared experiences that many outside the black community do not understand. The amount of time, effort, and money that is spent on black hair is not because of superficiality as some would have you believe; it's because black women know that the quality of their life and how others will treat them is riding on the presentation of their hair. And if we're going to dabble in real talk, the simple truth is that black women sporting natural hair deal with more bullshit than black women with straight hair or the adorable Julia Roberts curls of her ingenue years.

To be fair, people aren't always opposed to the natural look. For example, when Oprah graced the cover of *O* magazine wearing a three-and-a-half-pound Afro wig in 2012, she received nothing but positive feedback. But that's *Oprah*. And she was rocking a big-ass Afro on the cover of her *own* magazine, which is named after her. And it's a magazine that had ads for Pottery Barn wall sconces inside to counter-balance the Queen of Sheba vibes Oprah was serving with the 'fro. So, if anything, Oprah ended up doing the highly difficult and rarely achieved "straight-up black with a you-can-stop-clutching-your-purse-now-because-I'm-not-trying-to-start-a-revolution-that-will-be-televised-I'm-just-trying-to-get-retweeted-by-my-fans" look.

For all of us black women who are not #Blessed to be Oprah, we don't have the luxury of being celebrated when rocking natural hairstyles. You've probably noticed the examples: E!'s entertainment reporter Giuliana Rancic "joking" that singer/actress Zendaya must smell like weed because she was wearing dreadlocks; Blue Ivy Carter, Beyoncé and Jay Z's daughter, being dogged on social media because her hair isn't straight; comedian and cohost of *The Talk* Sheryl Underwood, who is black, flat-out stating that Afro hair is nasty. Yikes. I could keep going, but if I mention each and every time black women are slammed for their natural hair, I'll end up being sadder than I was watching the ending of *My Girl*. When black women's (and girls') hair does not meet beauty standards, they are bombarded with negativity that can cause feelings of self-doubt, shame, embarrassment, and confusion about who they should try to be and whether it's better to fully be themselves or not. Now, that doesn't mean that if a black woman straightens her hair, she doesn't have self-worth, or is trying to be white. That's a tired argument typically implemented by a woke black person who does his faux-deep version of the Fetty Wap triple greeting of "Hey, what's up, hello": "Sister, queen, goddess, don't you know what the white man is doing to you? You should wear your natural curls like a crown." Whenever I hear that, I always think, *Oh, shaddup. Just because you wear Buddhist beads doesn't mean you're enlightened.* But yet, this kind of gentle admonishment is said to black women way too often, so let's clear this up right now:

If a black woman straightens her hair, it doesn't mean she's rejecting her blackness. Sometimes a black lady wants her hair straightened because it looks cute that way, or she just wants to switch it up, or sometimes... well... OK. Take a seat, because what I'm about to tell you is a BPS, aka a Black People Secret.

For the uninitiated, a Black People Secret can fall under one, or be a combination of, the following categories:

1. Classified information that is kept under wraps for fear of cultural appropriation or judgment by society at large.

2. Something that's common knowledge within the black community but not society at large.

3. A fact that black people would openly acknowledge if so many non-black people weren't vocal about said fact in the first place.

I'll give you an example. All BPs know that Ice Cube can't act; however, we can't say anything because sites like Rotten Tomatoes have made it clear that his films are the equivalent of a bushel of bruised apples found in a back alley of a Trader Joe's. So now black people go on the offensive and effusively support him like he's that kid with bad eye-hand coordination who keeps swinging and a-missing during a game of T-ball. We're like, "Don't worry! Here's a pat on the back. Let me buy you a slice of ice-cream cake from Dairy Queen. Bless your heart." I don't know about other black people, but I don't want to condescend to a grown-ass man like I'm a Southern debutante. What I really want is to say, "Stop the madness, Mr. Cube! Every time I spend two hours watching one of your movies, that's time I can't spend writing my erotic fan-fiction novel entitled *The New Reparations*, which consists of detailed descriptions of *Scandal*'s President Fitz greasing Olivia Pope's scalp." But neither other BPs nor I can say this because everyone else won't shut the hell up about Cube's lack of acting talent, so we have to, as Bruce Springsteen once sang, "Take care of our own."

Now that you know what a Black People Secret is, I can explain why sometimes a black lady may straighten her hair. If she is anything like me, her natural hair has special shapeshifting qualities of epic T-1000 proportions, which means it has a mind of its own. For instance, when I sport an Afro, I may want to relax by sitting on my bed and leaning my head against the wall. When I get up from that spot, my hair has assumed the shape of said wall:

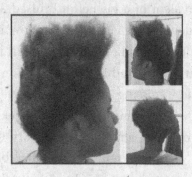

Yep. What was once a light, airy, and fluffy Afro has turned into a condensed mass of tightly coiled locks that resembles fiberglass insulation used on *House Hunters Renovation*. Forgive me for not having the exact wording down for this particular scientific phenomenon, but I believe it's called: That's Some Damn Bullshit. Just in case you're like, "Calm down, Pheebs. It's no biggie. You're still cute," let me tell you a little something about myself in order to put things into perspective for you. Not only will I unironically wear culottes, but I will also pose in pictures while rocking them with the swag of Georgey Dubs in the famous painting *Washington Crossing the*

Delaware. Clearly, I have confidence, alright? But I reach my limit of fierceness when, while relaxing in the comfort of my own home, my hair is *twisting* into itself until it's knotted like a pile of tangled iPhone earphones. Do you want to know what happens when my hair looks jacked up like that? Dudes stop trying to tap this and my dating life dries up. And if my dating life dries up, my vajeen will get covered in vines and moss like Edie Bouvier Beale's house in *Grey Gardens*. I can't live my life like that and neither can the thousands upon thousands of other black women whose natural hair suffers from this sort of shrinkage. So say it with me: "That's some damn bullshit!"

Ergo, black women's penchant for perming/ relaxing/ straightening their hair. But this was not the concern that I, nor other black women, had when they started straightening their hair at an early age. So let's go back in time *Quantum Leap*–style and see exactly what Yung Pheebs (which is coincidentally my rap handle) thought of her hair.

If, as a kid, I had a *While You Were Sleeping*–type head injury and a doctor was testing to see if I had amnesia, he wouldn't have to ask me to identify myself or name the current president. He'd simply need to have my mom show me a hot comb, and instantly, I'd answer, "It's Sunday. 8:59 p.m. *Living Single* is about to come on. My mom has to straighten my hair so I won't go to school tomorrow looking like Frederick Douglass." This scenario may seem strange to the average person, but I guarantee that most, if not all, black women my age and older could be tested this way. Sure, the details may be different—swap out *Living Single* for *Hangin' with Mr. Cooper,* and Sojourner Truth as the go-to reference instead of Frederick—but the point remains the same: From a very early age, the experience that most black girls have is one in which their hair is transformed from its natural state.

When I see the pictures of me, pre–hot comb, with Afro puffs, nothing registers. No memories come rushing back, which is a shame because those important formative years where I could've gotten acquainted with one of the most controversial signifiers of my blackness—my natural hair—without negative outside influence are forever lost. For me, there is only AHC: After Hot Comb. I was only six years old when my mom started straightening my hair. Every week, Mama Robinson would place a hot comb on the stove, and I'd sit down on a stack of telephone books—remember those?—waiting for it to heat up. The comb looked like a relic from an Earth, Wind & Fire tour and smelled like the *entire* hair-care line at Walgreens. Once the comb was hot like a pancake griddle, I'd snuggle between her legs and she'd get to work. I'd go on talking about whatever it is six-year-olds talk about (Dr. Seuss?), and every once in a while, I'd wince, and she'd go, "You have to sit still so you don't get burned." Yeah. If you're thinking that's a lot of responsibility for a very young person—to stay still as a piping-hot piece of metal hovers mere inches away from your scalp—you are correct. Getting little burns on my temples hurt like a mofo and was not a good look for school. After my hair was straightened, she would put it in cornrows or braids, painstakingly making it look perfect. Like a bartender tops off a Shirley Temple with a cherry and an orange wedge, my mom would finish off my braids with cute little barrettes from Sally Beauty Supply store. Aww, right? I mean, when you are rocking braids with tiny bear-shaped barrettes, it's hard not to be, as Beyoncé sang, "feelin' myself."

And to be fair, I'm not just bragging. I *was* a cute kid. Check my stats: My go-to ensemble was OshKosh B'gosh overalls, Disney-themed T-shirts, and Keds sneakers. My smile? Helen of Troy–esque, except instead of starting wars, it charmed adults. Add in the expert hair job my mom did, and we're talking straight-up catnip for *The Mickey Mouse Club* or *Kids Incorporated*. These years, the grade school years, are what I use as my Exhibits A–Z in the case of *Robinson Could Have Been a Child Model If Her Parents Got It Together v. Everyone Else Who Says the Exact Same Thing about Themselves*. To illustrate my point:

I mean… I was such a cute little kid that if I were up for adoption, Angelina Jolie surely would've snagged me.

That self-confidence only blossomed into full-blown delusion as I got older. Eventually, the braids were replaced by a bob cut with bangs that had the presence Tina Yothers's bangs did at her peak during *Family Ties*. *Wait till these white boys at my new school get a whiff of me*, I'd tell myself as I got dressed in the morning. Oh, they definitely did. And if Calvin Klein were to bottle that odor, it would have been called: Eau de Weary Grandmother at Post Office Who Hums a Negro Spiritual Parfum. Rolls off the tongue, doesn't it? To make matters worse, I often paired my asexual hairdo with lived-in black dress shoes, pleated khakis, and a primary-colored turtleneck from Eddie Bauer. At best, this outfit could be described as "Jehovah Witness Chic," and at worst, "recent Heaven's Gate defector." This, my friends, was the milk shake that did not bring all the boys to the yard. It was the milk shake that made them go, "You know, I'm really not into dairy right now. Or gluten. Or literally anything else that Phoebe Robinson is about." But in their defense (and mine), I grew up in Cleveland, Ohio, where most, if not all, black women and girls simultaneously looked like a twenty-five-year-old new-hire local weatherwoman and a seventy-five-year-old anchorwoman signing off for the last time after four decades in the business. So my aesthetic during these years is somewhat forgivable, yet also? Unforgettable.

Recently, I've started to question my deep fondness over my childhood looks. A lot of my self-love during that time was tied to my hair being manipulated to mimic that of white people's. Not that that was necessarily my or my mom's intentions, but looking like everyone else made me feel good. Fitting in, especially when you're a kid and don't realize that standing out is the way to go, was important. It's necessary for survival in school. Not that I was bullied—I wasn't—but knowing that straightening my hair wasn't going to cause any nega-tive attention or elicit a "*What's that*?" surely brought me relief. You know the teenage edict: Fly below the radar. Assimilate.

The middle school years are, hands down, the most critical in my understanding of my hair because that's when I upgraded from my mom using a hot comb on my head to having my hair professionally straightened, aka getting a perm or a relaxer. This was the big leagues, which meant that getting my hair done was no longer a fun, if sometimes painful, bonding time with my mom. I was now in the hands of a trained professional who introduced me to "creamy crack." For the uninitiated, creamy crack is code for the chemicals used to straighten / perm kinky hair. My hair was going to finally look like those black ladies I saw on TV: Perfect. Shiny. Straight. Unfortunately, my permed hair was less *Jet* magazine "Beauty of the Week" and more "Little Rock Nine," aka a chaste chin-length cut with a tightly curled bang and a headband. It's the perfect do for when saying "I'm a virgin" simply requires too much effort.

I quickly learned that getting a perm was serious business. There were a lot of rules that came along with relaxing my hair. I had to have a scarf on hand at all times in case it rained, otherwise my hair would turn kinky again and ruin what my mom just paid for. Similarly, getting my hair wet while showering was *no bueno*. The solution? Donning a shower cap that made my head look like a package of popped Jiffy Pop popcorn. Also, sweating was not encouraged, so yes to half-assing it in gym class and double yes to full-assing it on the couch, watching *Boy Meets World*. Oh! Forgot to mention. There was absolutely, positively, no scratching my scalp because if I did, when I would get my hair relaxed again later, the chemicals from the perm would sting the areas, causing a scab to form. "Aaah!" exclaimed my ex-boyfriend, a high school teacher, after I explained this to him a few years ago. "I was wondering why I only saw black girls doing this. Didn't want to think it was a 'black' thing." No, babe, you were right; patting our heads like they're the bottoms of ketchup bottles is indeed a black thing.

Because getting a perm at a hair salon is a long process that eats up many hours on a Saturday, I learned that having a weekend was a white thing. My white classmates would regale me with tales of doing things like going to the movies, playing in the park, eating fast food. Then it'd be my turn: "Well, I went to the hair salon for most of Saturday. And it was mostly boring except for every once in a while a mom would say to her kids, 'Sit your black ass down and act like you got some sense.'"

"Oh… cool," the white kids would respond with looks that were a combination of disappointment and confusion, like when a recent college graduate's parents come to visit but don't bring any groceries, so the grad's like, "Uhhhhh, I don't get it. Why are you here?" Fortunately, we were middle schoolers with the attention span of, well, middle schoolers, so this moment of awkwardness would quickly pass, and we resumed caring about nothing but raging hormones. Except, over time, I slowly began to care more and more about my hair. While I never used the term explicitly, I would sit in class and determine which girls had "good hair."

First, there were the black girls with the thick, long majestic manes. No matter how straight my hair got, I knew my hair was never going to be like theirs. My hair was always going to be fine. Not like "Ooooh, look at Oscar Isaac. He's *fiiiiiiiiiine*." I mean, "fine" like thin. Not sturdy. What Sally Fields's bones would be like if she wasn't taking hella amounts of Boniva. And then there were the girls with baby hairs. If you're unfamiliar with the expression, Google baby hairs' most popular ambassadors, Rozonda Thomas, aka the C in R&B supergroup TLC, and Jennifer Lopez when she was still Jenny from the Block. To me, baby hairs hit that sweet spot of being straight enough to be easily combed, yet ethnic enough that I didn't feel like I was turning my back on my blackness. I definitely lusted for that. But there was this one classmate who seemed like the perfect representation of "good hair." Her skin was the color of light brown sugar, and her hair color matched. It looked so silky smooth that I bet she was able to do her hair in the time it took to heat up a Pop-Tart. But the best part? Every once in a while, she would have flyaways—you know, when an unruly few hairs stick out from the rest of your hair? I envied that, because no matter how much I relaxed my hair, I knew that in its natural state, it could never do that. I would never pause a game of indoor volleyball to quickly tuck a flyaway behind my ear. Nor would my hair ever move effortlessly in the breeze; instead, it would stand still like a villain atop a building, surveying Gotham City. Its rigidness was a reminder that my hair was not the *good hair* that a hairdresser could easily comb through; mine would have to be tugged along like a *Real World/Road Rules Challenge* contestant being dragged across the finish line. This light-brown-sugar-colored black girl with her hair seamlessly pulled back into a ponytail? No gel to slick down the sides? Man, I thought she was the cat's pajamas. I wished I was her. I wished I had her good hair. Why?

I figured life would be easier if my hair wasn't kinky. I hated that I had to change it in order for it to be considered good in the first place. I hated that the process to change it hurt. I hated that no matter how many relaxers I got, my hair never looked as good as the light-brown-sugar girl's hair. I didn't want to have to spend my time worrying about whether my hair got wet, lest the nappy hair multiply like Gremlins do when they are exposed to water. But even more than that, I assumed that if I had better hair, I would finally get my first boyfriend. That people would think I was pretty. I know, I know. It makes me cringe to type that, but it was my truth at the time. The fact that I did not look like the light-brown-sugar-colored girl + I did not have her good hair + I did not get the attention she got = I must have not been pretty. Damn. The math we tell ourselves sometimes. This "good hair" obsession became glaringly obvious once I started attending Gilmour Academy, my predominantly white private high school.

During my four years at Gilmour, there were only two black girls in the entire school, and neither were in my grade. Being the only black girl in your high school graduating class is… weird. Oh, you probably thought I was going to make a joke to lighten the moment. Not this time; this time I'm being completely sincere. Being the only black girl in my grade was fucking weird. I mean, I made friends. I was a bit of a class clown. And what do you know? When I wasn't being a complete slacker and turned in my homework, my teachers actually liked me! Huh. Still, despite those positives, there was always a tinge of loneliness that colored my high school experience. I didn't have a mirror, a soundboard, someone who knew the same things I did because we were from the same cultural tribe. Someone who knew the extent of the lie that was my permed hair. Someone who felt they had also been set up to fail because their straight hair was never going to be straight like the white girls in class. Someone who every six to eight weekends lost their Saturday to a hair salon.

Above all, I wished I had a friend who could help me make sense of how my brother had the completely opposite high school experience than me. See, my brother was a senior when I was a freshman at Gilmour, and he was Mr. Popular. All the teachers loved him—and yes, I know, it's because he did all his homework and did it well, but shut up—he was in all of the clubs, and importantly, *every* girl loved him. On the other hand, no one wanted to date me, lanky with my stupid Little Rock Nine hair. Sure, I made the boys laugh, but high school boys do not pitch a tent in their pants because of your flawless impression of your algebra teacher. Instead, they give you a four-year, all-expenses-paid trip to the Friend Zone, which includes having riveting conversations about how the chicken tenders at lunch taste, watching girls who are objectively way better looking than you command their attention, and not going to your junior prom, which took place on a boat, which you use as your excuse for not attending, when in actuality, you freakin' love boats, BUT NO ONE ASKED YOU TO THE PROM AND DAMN IF YOU ARE GOING TO BE THE ONLY BLACK PERSON AT THE PROM WITHOUT A DATE AND WATCH ALL THESE WHITE PEOPLE BE ALL IN LOVE AND LUST WITH EACH OTHER WHILE YOU SIT BY YOURSELF OR WITH THE WAITSTAFF ON THE BOAT, WHO WILL ABSO-MOTHERFUCKIN-LUTELY BE OLD-ASS BLACK DUDES WITH OLD-ASS BLACK DUDE NAMES LIKE REGINALD OR VERNON OR HAYWOOD OR ANYTHING THAT REMINDS YOU OF TREES AND SHARECROPPING. Damn all that, so my alibi was *I don't like boats.*

But I LOVE boats. They are so opulent, so fanciful! When they pick up speed, and your hair gets tossed around, you can pretend to be Beyoncé! And if you move your hand up and down and pretend like you're singing, you get to be Mariah Carey! That's right: You can be Bey *and* Mimi in the span of a few seconds! I also love that when other people see you on boats, they think your life is literally cunnilingus from unicorns, and even though that's not the case, you're still like, "Yep! Pretty much!" And oh! I haven't even mentioned my number one reason for loving boats: the "Jenny from the Block" music video. You remember that moment in the video when she and former fiancé Ben Affleck are chilling on a boat? She's lying down like a queen, and he's rubbing on her booty and gives it a tender peck like the kind Charlie gave his golden ticket before he went off to visit the Chocolate Factory. I mean!!!!! A hot dude rubbing your booty the way Bobby Flay puts spice rub on a slab of ribs, and then kissing your donk as if to say, "I know I do not deserve any of this or you, so I'm going to literally kiss your ass and then metaphorically kiss it later on" was and continues to be #RelationshipGoals, #BoatGoals, and #LifeGoals for me. Who cares that J. Lo and Ben broke up? The point is boats are all about fantasy, and as a lanky black girl with not-perfect hair, I fell in love with fantasy. I needed fantasy because real life was not as fun or fabulous. Being the sole black girl in my class who no guy, black or white, thought was pretty or worthy of special attention was a lonely, seemingly never-ending experience—and it was all my hair's fault, I was sure of it.

Yep. I truly thought my hair was why I wasn't special, and why I didn't have a date to the junior prom. But who could I tell this to? I didn't have that black girl sitting beside me in class every day who would understand my insecurities. And sure, I probably could've talked about this with my mom, but to the teenaged brain, talking about feelings with a parent is a fate worse than death. So, yep, I told myself *I don't like boats. That's my story and I'm sticking to it.* And, lovely reader, not only did I say I don't like boats, but I further buried my feelings by acting snooty about junior prom with my classmates. "You know, prom just feels like really a thing for seniors." "I mean, if you go to junior prom, then doesn't it make senior prom less special?" "What could possibly be *gained* from a junior prom?" And then I laughed and laughed and laughed all by myself and all the way home to my bedroom, where I could escape into my TV.

Movies and TV shows were my friends and where I first saw the not stereotypically "cool" girls and women have infinitely cooler lives than me. It's where I witnessed C. J. Cregg, the brainiac White House press secretary, kick ass at her job on *The West Wing*, with no shortage of men who were interested in her. It's where I watched *Living Single*'s Maxine Shaw with her awesome braids be a successful lawyer and kick it with her awesome black bestie girlfriends who always had her back. It's where I saw Felicity Porter on *Felicity* find her true passion in life during college (art), while also watching her be at the heart of a love triangle between two guys who couldn't get enough of her awkwardness. Sure, all three of these women are pretty in their own right, but they did not lead with the pretty. People loved them because they were awesome. Because they said the smart thing.

Because they said the funny thing. These ladies and many more gave this lanky black girl hope. And then during my senior year of high school, that hope turned into a game plan, when I saw a music video for the song "They-Say Vision" by a singer named Res.

As soon as I saw Res, I was like, *who is this kick-ass woman*? This bare-midriffed, dark-chocolate-colored beauty who sang a hybrid of rock/hip-hop music all while sporting the most magnificent dreadlocks. Like what the what? She was alternative. She didn't fit in. She wasn't *trying* to fit in. And best of all? She was *really* fucking pretty with her natural hair. I knew that it was *possible* to rock the natural look; I had seen women like Brandy and Lauryn Hill do it in the mainstream media. But to me, those women always reminded me of the extremely pretty and popular girls in high school. But Res? She never got the praise or attention that she deserved, despite being gorgeous and talented. She became an underdog hero to me.

Oh, I can do that? I thought when I looked at Res. I mean, there was another way? I didn't have to go get a relaxer? I didn't have to hate my hair? I was just so bowled over by Res. I immediately bought her debut album *How I Do* and studied the CD booklet that accompanied it. The most striking image in it was a black-and-white photo of her looking over her shoulder as she was walking away from the camera. *When I go to college, I'm going to look like this. I'm going to have dreads, and I'm going to look over my shoulder like this whether it is necessary to do so or not.* I was set. It was time for me to love my hair like Res loved hers. Bye-bye, relaxer!

It was at that moment that I made a choice: I was not going to start the next chapter of my life in New York City feeling horrible about my hair and the way it looked. I was excited, but also a little nervous, to tell my mom that I was done straightening my hair. Considering she had either straightened my hair for me or paid someone else to do it for eleven years, I was worried that she would think it was a rejection of the way she raised me. But she didn't. She was #DoYouBoo before #DoYouBoo was a thing that people said in the world. Mama Robinson was on board and agreed that after I graduated high school I could stop perming my hair. I was relieved, and I think my mom was, too. After all, I had not proven that I was the most responsible teenager, so she was probably thankful that I wasn't going to have to find a hairdresser on my own and get to the salon every eight weeks between studies and work. And I think there was a small part of her that was happy that I was making my own decision. She and my dad raised me to be an independent thinker, and there's no way she would have wanted me to straighten my hair to make *her* happy.

A few months later, I found myself at the hair salon again with my mom. I told the hairdresser that I was going off to college in New York, and I was going natural.

The hairdresser congratulated me, and told me the first step was that she had to cut off all of my processed and damaged hair, of which there was quite a bit. In fact, there was so much damage that what was left of my hair was not strong enough to start dreads just yet. But in the meantime, the hairdresser told me, I could have some fake hair braided into mine to rock cornrows for the summer. I was ecstatic. *Wait. Like Queen Latifah in* Set It Off*? You're telling me that I'm going to look like a badass, which is something I have never been in life up until this point? Sign me up!* Who knew that I could be this happy to see my own hair?!?! I had seen it processed all these years and felt like a fraud. But seeing *my* hair in its natural state? Duuuuuuuuuuuuuuude. I might be just as cool as Res. DUDE! I'm going to be looking over my shoulder AF all the time. I'm going to be that cool-but-people-haven't-hipped-to-how-cool-I-am-yet cool. I'm going to keep leading with my dope personality. I'm going to be underrated and still carry on because I know how dope I am. I'm going to like my hair because it feels *authentic*. And that's when that equation in my head, that value I placed on myself, started to change. It became: Me, the lanky brown-skinned girl + my real and good hair (good because it's a part of me) + giving a middle finger to societal standards of beauty = I might be pretty. Sometimes the math we tell ourselves checks out.

It took some time, but at the age of eighteen, I finally got acquainted with what my real hair felt and looked like. And it's held some surprises. My curls coil tightly, and when I angle my head just right in the light, a few streaks of strawberry blond and red hair can be seen on one side of my head. That's something that was passed down to me from my dad. I learned that my hair is also kind of hard to comb through sometimes, which can be annoying, but I like it. It's not easy, but *I'm* not easy, so we match. I can do lot of things with it: braid it, dread it, 'fro it, curl it. I can establish a kinship with other black people who wear their hair this way. Our hair becomes a language that only we speak. It took some time, but I realize I have been fluent in it all this time. And now I have so much more to say. It started as "I think I might be pretty" and "I think I might not hate myself anymore," and slowly the "might" fell away—and I do mean *slowly*. But finally, I love myself and my hair, and when I look over my shoulder, I'm not doing it like Res anymore. I'm doing it like me.

A Brief History of Black Hair in Film, TV, Music, and Media

⌒

Black people are everywhere these days! On TV screens and magazine covers, headlining concert tours and dominating sports, making history in politics and being a definitive voice in the world of science (go, Neil deGrasse Tyson, go!). But what's really important is that black people's myriad *hairstyles* are everywhere. Lupita Nyong'o's go-to do, a low fade or a much chicer version of the Gumby side-part, is lusted after. Mary J. Blige is known for her signature platinum-blond locks. And the Weeknd's hair looks like a Museum of Modern Art installation piece made up of twigs and used pipe cleaners from a Halloween costume. Clearly, the options are endless, which is inspiring for a whole new generation of black kids.

This wasn't always the case. When I was growing up, there were typically three options for black women's hairstyles depicted in the media: 1. The bank teller style, aka shoulder-length, chemically straightened hair, 2. very long and very straight Pocahontas hair, or 3. if it needed to be clear that a character was *real black*, meaning they weren't a token black friend for white people, but had actual other black friends, a natural hairstyle like short dreadlocks was often paired with asexual clothing to show that this character cared a lot about Black History Month stamps and not much going to the bone zone. And before any of you black male readers laugh, things were just as dismal for you. Your options were the Old School Steve Harvey, a tightly groomed high-top fade that glistened like a homemade Styrofoam-and-glitter Christmas ornament, and the New School Steve Harvey, also known as the Bald As Fuck. Sure, Bruce Willis and Kojak are known for their cue balls, but black men continue to have this look on lock.

Now, thankfully, we're in the middle of a moment when there's less strict adherence to white Eurocentric beauty standards. As a result, black hair is less likely to be viewed, especially when in its natural state, as a political reaction to or rejection of white beauty. Witnessing this acceptance over time has encouraged me to embrace my own natural beauty, which I have wholeheartedly done. Ever since I told that hairdresser that I was going natural as a college-bound eighteen-year-old, I've been bald, had dreadlocks, a baby 'fro, a frohawk, *Moesha* braids, Senegalese twists, big, long fluffy hair that went down to my boobs, a regular-sized Afro, fauxlocks, and Janet Jackson *Velvet Rope* hair. It has clearly been quite the hair journey, not just for me but also society, so in honor of all the progress made, I want to take a look back at some

47

of the most influential and most memorable black hairstyles in film, TV, music, and media.

DOROTHY DANDRIDGE, 1954

With her light complexion (she was the daughter of two biracial parents), her European-looking features, and her straight hair, Dorothy Dandridge, alongside fellow singer/actress Lena Horne, was promoted by Hollywood as an acceptable face of black beauty during the industry's Golden Age. For black women, she was aspirational, and that was never truer than in her definitive role as the titular character in *Carmen Jones*. Dandridge played a heartbreaking vixen with short, dark cropped hair—a striking contrast to actresses like Lauren Bacall, Marilyn Monroe, and Grace Kelly, who were the look du jour with their flaxen hair. Dandridge stood out while letting the world know that black is beautiful.

LITTLE RICHARD, 1956
AND JAMES BROWN, 1960s

For a lot of young'uns, when they think of James Brown, the image that comes to mind is his 2004 mug shot, in which he was wearing a multicolored bathrobe and had unkempt chemically straightened hair. This look is known in the black community as everyone's auntie's "If I Have to Come Down These Stairs One Mo 'Gain Because You

Little Richard proves that the hashtag #BlackExcellence extends beyond talent and intelligence and also includes cheekbones so smooth they could also double as slalom skiing courses at the Winter Olympics.

Damn Kids Woke Me Up, I'mma Call *All* Your Mamas and End This Sleepover" look. As for Richard, people instantly think of his vocal tics—"*Whoo!*"—and his appearance in GEICO commercials in the early aughts. But both of these men brought to the mainstream a style that was known as the "conk" (derived from congolene, a hair straightener gel made from lye). Because this look required its wearers to endure its painful process, the do was seen as super masculine and served as a rite of passage from adolescence into adulthood for men. And thanks to folks like Little Richard and James Brown, it also became cool. In their later years, they each had their struggles, which dimmed their lights—Richard had financial disputes with his record label, while James began abusing PCP and had several domestic-abuse arrests—but there is no denying their impact on black hair and culture at large.

DIANA ROSS & THE SUPREMES, 1960s

Fun fact: All the fumes from the hair sheen that was sprayed on the Supremes' hair gave Ed Sullivan a contact high.

For those of you who are too young to remember Diana Ross & the Supremes, I'll explain them this way: If you combined the popularity of En Vogue, TLC, and Destiny's Child, then you'll have scratched the surface of how big Diana Ross & the Supremes were during their heyday. They were the premiere act of Motown Records during the 1960s, rivaled the Beatles in terms of popularity, and to date, they are still America's most successful vocal group, with twelve number one hits on the *Billboard* Hot 100 chart. And if these achievements weren't enough, their highly stylized and straightened wigs—ranging from bouffants to bobs and everything in between—were hugely influential on black women everywhere. Similar to how every time Kim Kardashian changes her hair, legions of fans lose their minds, every time Ross and the Supremes changed their look, people would talk about it, minus the whole part where trolls are like, "Hahaha! Remember that time you slept with a dude and videotaped it? We're going to judge you for it for the rest of your life." Black women looked to Diana Ross & the Supremes as a reflection of their best selves, which probably explains why throughout the course of the group's popularity, fans routinely asked them to wear their hair natural. But producer and founder of Motown Records Berry Gordy Jr. worried that doing that would alienate white audiences, so it never happened. Shame.

ANGELA DAVIS, 1970s

True story. Whenever I sport an Afro, strangers will ask me all sorts of ridiculous questions, such as the following:

> Dry Cleaner Employee: "Who are you dressing up as?"
> Me: "Uhhh, it's not Halloween; it's April."
> Dry Cleaner Employee: "So, not Foxxy Cleopatra?"
> Me: "Keep my clothes forever!!! Bye!!!"

Then I race out of the dry cleaners, abandoning my classy Banana Republic sweaters the way baby Penguin was abandoned at the beginning of *Batman Returns*. Aww, that took a turn. Anyway, the point is these kinds of awkward encounters happen, but thankfully, they are few and far between, because most folks recognize that I wasn't wearing a "costume" but was just being myself. And I have Angela Davis to thank for that, because she and her Afro are, by far, some of the biggest symbols of black self-love, the civil rights movement, and challenging the status quo.

Remember in 1994 when figure skater Tonya Harding had her then-husband attack Nancy Kerrigan with a billy club, and Nancy let out that infamous cry of *"Why!"* that was *so good* that even Mary J. Blige would've been like, "Damn, I need to get some soul like that!" That *"Why!"* is pretty much how many white people reacted to this era of black pride, and in particular Davis and her 'fro. The 'fro became a powerful political sign of the wearer embracing their African ancestry and rejecting long-held beauty ideals. Because Davis embraced her individuality, fiercely bucked against dominant hair trends of the time—often pairing her Afro with a raised fist in the air—and was highly vocal in her quest for gender equality, much of mainstream America viewed her as threatening and aggressive. But to many black men and women, she was a reminder that, above all, they should love themselves despite what society deems to be the ideal. Furthermore, her 'fro inspired others to sport theirs as a visible expression of their self-love. This newfound confidence in self-expression not only encouraged men and women to speak up about their hair and what blackness meant to them but also to fight for civil rights and other issues affecting people of color. In short, Angela Davis helped usher in a time when the black community had officially reached Super Saiyan levels of confidence (#DragonBallZFanForLife), and since then we haven't looked back.

CICELY TYSON'S CORNROWS IN THE TV DRAMA
EAST SIDE/WEST SIDE, 1973

It's pretty safe to say that Cicely is one of the co-founders of the phrase You mad? after she "shocked" white America by sporting a popular African-American hairstyle on primetime television.

In 1979, Bo Derek wore cornrows in the movie *10*, and as a result, this hairstyle became insanely popular in mass culture. But let's be real: This was a look that was as common in the black community as *Soul Train* dance lines. Every black girl who was raised by her mama or grandma had been wearing her hair this way to church, school, and the playground for years, and the first real portrayal of this hairstyle in media came way before Bo. Thanks to Cicely Tyson in the 1973 TV series *East Side/West Side*, America was exposed to, and quite possibly shocked by, this African-American–centric look. Prior to Cicely Tyson, black women on TV were only seen wearing sleek bob cuts or sky-high bouffants, but Cicely broke the trend and opened up the world's eyes to what black hair could look like. Furthermore, because she was and still is such a revered actress, the cornrows styling on her was seen as acceptable to mainstream America and opened the door for more black women to wear their hair naturally.

GRACE JONES'S FLATTOP, 1980

I believe Grace Jones might quite possibly be the most influential figure for black female beauty. Sure, the everyday black woman is far less boundary-pushing than Jones, but her impact can be seen everywhere. Her pioneering style is all over black women fashion boards on Pinterest; her message of individuality is echoed in the style of left-of-center celebs like Janelle Monáe and Zoë Kravitz; and her "I'm sexy because I terrify and challenge gender norms" fingerprint can be seen on anyone in the mainstream who is androgynous. And there is no better symbol of Jones's influence than in her flattop haircut, a style that is heavily in vogue today. This traditionally masculine hairstyle (known as the Kid 'n Play) is a fuck-you in the face of societal standards. It wasn't meant to turn men on; instead, it was an extension of her artistic expression. Grace, after all, is an artist, something that society conveniently forgets that black women can be. Well, Grace *demanded* the attention, making it so that people couldn't look away and instead had to confront, accept, and, finally, be in awe of her art and beauty. And she is the ultimate badass because of it.

OLA RAY IN "THRILLER" MUSIC VIDEO, 1982

I'm pretty sure if you look up *nailing it* in UrbanDictionary. com, you'd see a picture of Ms. Ola Ray rocking this do. Her Jheri curl mullet in this video glistened like a rotisserie chicken at Boston Market. And that level of shine, my friends, is something we should aspire to. I'm talking about glistening like you ought to be accompanied by two sides and a biscuit. #ShineGoals. But in all seriousness, the Jheri curl is generally remembered for being worn by popular black men like the rappers in N.W.A, singers Lionel Richie and Rick James, and actors such as Eriq La Salle, so the fact that a woman sported it in one of the most popular music videos of all time made other black women feel more comfortable with adopting this look for themselves.

AUNT JEMIMA MAKEOVER, 1989

Aww, Aunt Jemima is cute here! She looks the type of black lady who makes sure to put your Thanksgiving leftovers in the indestructible home of two paper plates because she doesn't trust that you're going to return her Tupperware.
And she's right. You won't.

OK, it may seem a little strange of me to give kudos to this look, but hear me out. The original image of Aunt Jemina was of an old black lady wearing a jankity head scarf that made Harriet Tubman's dirty head scarves—which were dirty because she was *working the Underground Railroad*—look like they were specialty handmade pieces from Anthropologie. That, my friends, is *no bueno*. The old Aunt Jemima image was an offensive, racist bowl of boo-boo, which is why the 1989 makeover was long overdue and necessary.

The new Aunt Jemima looks like a black lady whose end-of-the-world survival kit includes bottled water, recipes for her collard greens and mac and cheese, and all her Barry White vinyls. In short, she looks like every black mom in America, and that is a motherfucking upgrade that I shall celebrate for the rest of my days.

JANET JACKSON *POETIC JUSTICE* BRAIDS, LENNY KRAVITZ "ARE YOU GONNA GO MY WAY" DREADS, 1993

Janet Jackson serves her most "Why are you coming home at 2 a.m. smelling like cheap perfume from Rite Aid?" face. I have spent the better part of my adult life trying to master this, to no avail.

I'm grouping Janet's braids and Lenny's dreads together because they both fall under the "stay woke" category.

For the uninitiated, "stay woke" is when a black person is informed of the world's injustices and how those injustices affect the black community, and then they let *everybody* know that they are informed. Sometimes the "I'm woke and staying woke" memo is as simple as a person changing their name to something more Afrocentric, or wearing bow ties in kente cloth. Other times you are clued into their wokeness by the frequency with which they light candles and incense all over their crib like Angela Bassett did in the Buddhist-praying scene in *What's Love Got to Do with It*. Or how they continually drop quotes from *The Autobiography of Malcolm X* when all anyone else in the room wants to do is watch *The Voice*. But by far, the biggest sign of a newly stay woke person is that person starting to wear his or her hair naturally, especially in dreads or braids.

Stay wokeness was at an all-time high during the '90s. During this time, there was a litany of TV shows (*A Different World*), movies (*Do the Right Thing*), and music (the entire neo-soul genre) featuring conscious brothers and sistas who were providing commentary on the black experience. And if you want to know what a quintessential stay woke person is, then you don't have to look any further than Janet Jackson's character in *Poetic Justice*. First of all, her lawyer mom named her Justice because naming her "Something Black People Don't Always Get in a Court of Law" would have been too on the nose. Secondly, she is a poet who does natural hair on the side.

If I could go back in time and lose my virginity to anyone, it would be Lenny Kravitz. Oh, sorry, were you expecting me to say something about his hair?

Lastly, she sports braids, which any writer during the '90s will tell you is shorthand for "bitch is an insomniac, that's how woke she is." And just as many black women of the '90s were rocking braids to show how conscious they were, lots of '90s black dudes were pulling a Lenny Kravitz and wearing dreadlocks. Not only do dreads celebrate the rejection of mainstream beauty standards, but they also have the added bonus of illustrating how spiritual the wearer is (it is believed that spiritual energies usually exit the body through the top of the head, so if the hair is knotted or dreaded, the energy stays in the hair and body). And for those guys who aren't as spiritual… well, they might have worn dreads to attract hot, stay woke black women who would not give up the good-good unless these dudes talked about religion a lot and decorated their houses with black Santa Clauses.

HALLE BERRY'S PIXIE CUT, 1994

Although this dream pales in comparison to MLK's dream, mine is to one day remake the rom-com America's Sweethearts in which Berry and I would take on the Catherine Zeta-Jones and Julia Roberts roles as rival sisters… because that would mean that a bunch of movie studio executives believed that I could ever be related to someone this hot.

Simply put, this is the "Rachel" haircut for black people. When Halle debuted this, every black lady wanted this look, and then they all proceeded to *get* that look. Which was great except for one key component: They didn't have the Halle Berry face or body to match. So while this hairstyle helped launch Halle's career into the stratosphere and made her the ultimate sex symbol, the rest of the black ladies with this look were still busy shopping at JCPenney and waiting for dudes to call them back on their landlines. But they looked cute waiting, though, and that's all that mattered.

MICHAEL JORDAN, 1995

Let's all remember Jordan when he was at his best: the pre-Hitler-mustache-wearing days of the 2000s. Seriously, does he have no black friends who would point at the 'stache and go, "Bruh? Da fuq?"

MJ had been beloved for quite a while at this point, but the mid-'90s were his peak in terms of popularity. He had just won his fourth NBA championship, starred in *Space Jam*, and had tons of endorsement contracts. He was killing it. In fact, he was killing it so hard that he was probably the *one* black dude straight white women could publicly acknowledge that they wanted to bone, and their husbands would two-thumbs-up it *Siskel & Ebert*–style. And to top it all off, because he had been sporting the bald look during his rise to the top as one of the greatest athletes of all time, he became a style icon that every black dude tried to emulate. And who could blame them? MJ was rich, the epitome of cool, and everyone from Oprah to McDonald's (corporations are people, too, ya know) loved him. So it's no wonder black guys mimicked him. OK, maybe part of the reason why some black dudes like my dad shaved their heads is because they were going bald and didn't want to look like *In Living Color*'s Homey the Clown. Whatever the case may be, the cue ball look became one of the most popular styles of the '90s for black men, thanks to people like Jordan.

ERYKAH BADU, 1997

As soon as Badu rocked her sky-high and colorful head wraps in the music video for her single "On & On," it seemed every woman of color tried to copy this signature look. The style was radical because it marked a turn away from the bone-straight hairstyles that dominated black hair culture at that time. Badu, along with other neo-soul musicians of that era, including Maxwell, D'Angelo, and Jill Scott, made waves because they openly embraced their natural hair stories. Essentially, these folks helped usher in the next great wave for the natural hair industry, and Badu was at the forefront.

Badu's uniqueness was warmly accepted from the get-go, and she achieved massive mainstream success.

If I had to be birthed out of anyone else's vajeen besides my mom's, it would be Erykah Badu's. I just feel like it's the perfect combo of all-natural Earth Mother nurturing and swag-filled "I ain't got time for these fools."

Along the way, she inspired plenty of women to experiment and embrace their own unique styles—or, more realistically, if they were like me, they simply copied what Badu did until they discovered their *own* best look. Of course, I never looked as chic when rocking the head wraps; I looked like I was smuggling a Swiffer WetJet, walking out of Target. But that's no matter, because the important thing is that Badu, like Angela Davis, inspired so many black women to not be afraid to wear their hair any way that they chose.

LAURYN HILL, LATE '90s

There is so much to say about this woman! She's an icon! A musical genius! Complicated and troubled! Someone who can shoot people in the heart just by singing a few gut-wrenching notes! Above all, Hill is a *pioneer*: the first woman nominated in ten different GRAMMY categories and the first woman to win five of the awards in one night. And media *loved* her—she made the cover of *Time* and was voted one of *People*'s 50 Most Beautiful People. She did all of this while rocking some pretty bomb-ass dreadlocks, which is absolutely part of the reason why I wore dreadlocks in college. Thanks, Lauryn!

CHRIS ROCK'S DOCUMENTARY
GOOD HAIR, 2009

Similar to how some white people watched *The Wire* and felt as though they knew everything about urban life, many white peeps believed they had black hair all figured out after viewing Rock's 2009 documentary. And, sure, they became well versed in the basics: You're not supposed to touch a black woman's hair after she gets it permed; black women will, through the course of a lifetime, spend hundreds of thousands of dollars on styling; and black women clutch shower caps in their hands with the same fervor priests do rosary beads in an exorcism movie. I'd go as far as to argue that more than any other movie, *Good Hair* has educated the masses about black hair in a profound way. But still, that doesn't mean that it taught people everything. There are many black hair secrets that weren't covered, and in case you're wondering, I'm not going to divulge them here either. Not because I fear being murdered by the keepers of the BPSs. Oh no, there are repercussions far worse than taking an eternal dirt nap—like walking down the streets of New York City and every old black lady giving me the stank eye because I opened my big fat mouth about black hair. Besides not being able to remember my log-in password on Seamless, having old black ladies be disappointed in me is pretty much the only thing that can make me Claire Danes ugly cry, y'all.

JANELLE MONÁE, 2012

You know how Steve Madden is totally fine with his line of products just being knock-offs of luxury brands? Well, I am the Steve Madden to Janelle Monáe's Christian Louboutin. When she came on the scene, I immediately incorporated more black-and-white ensembles into my wardrobe, and when she started wearing black patent shoes to red-carpet events, I ran out and found a pair of knock-offs and wore them to every special event instead of heels. I'm not the only one who has done this, so clearly, Monáe is a trendsetter for many black women and girls, and hopefully will remain that way

Janelle Monáe's poof is so on point that I would pay to live inside it and #RealTalk, it's bigger than my NYC apartment, so this is a win-win.

for the rest of her career. Yet, for me, I think the peak of her career will always be 2012. That year, Monáe became the first black woman sporting natural hair to land a campaign for a major cosmetics company. Monáe being a face for CoverGirl was a *game changer*. Not only did she provide a positive example for countless black girls and women, but by featuring her front and center on a national campaign, the makeup conglomerate was *finally* acknowledging that black women were a consumer buying base. And by doing so, they stepped up and expanded their color palette, so black women no longer had to Bob Ross their way into making a foundation that worked for them, aka combining a bunch of "close, but no cigar" shades together to get one color that matched their skin tone.

VIOLA DAVIS TAKING HER WIG OFF ON *HOW TO GET AWAY WITH MURDER*, 2014

Let me just start by stating that THIS IS THE SINGLE GREATEST MOMENT IN BLACK WOMEN TELEVISION HISTORY. Sorry, I don't mean to go caps lock on ya like that, but I really feel it is the only way to emphasize how important this moment was. Let me set the scene, and then you'll see why I'm not exaggerating. BTdubs, what I'm about to tell you is a major spoiler, so if you haven't seen season one of *How to Get Away with Murder*, read this at your own peril.

To set the scene: Annalise Keating (Viola Davis) is a high-powered lawyer with dubious morals, who has been married to her husband, Sam, for a long time. They're both cheating on each other, which isn't as trifling as it sounds. I mean, two people cheating on each other is like when you and a bestie both have New Year's resolutions to find better jobs and then on January 2, it all goes to shit because you both independently discover that there's a *Judge Joe Brown* marathon on TV and decide it's way more fun to watch that than it is to upload résumés to Monster.com. Then when you find out the other messed up, instead of getting mad, you just giggle and share a look like, "No one will ever get me the way that you do." What I'm getting at here is that Annalise and Sam both messed up, so it cancels out. That's how relationships work, right?

Anyway, while Sam was fooling around with a college student, Anna was hooking up with a superhot black cop who would show up to her job and go down on her, aka the man was a true American hero and every time he showed up on screen, I pledged my allegiance to him like he was the damn United States flag. These side relationships were going swimmingly until Sam knocked up his jump off and then, under mysterious circumstances, she was killed. Sam denied any wrongdoing, but when faced with incriminating evidence that would ruin his life, Annalise decides to call him out.

Here's a lesson to all of us: If you are going to confront your cheating husband with the greatest nine-word question in television history—*"Why is your penis in a dead girl's phone?"*—you want to have your wig off when you say it. Because no matter what his answer is going to be, it's only going to piss you off and make you want to fight, and you can't fight if you're too worried about your wig getting snatched like a white teenage girl in a Lifetime movie. So you must take the wig off and carefully hang it somewhere the way Jews delicately hang a mezuzah outside their homes to protect those inside it. And that's exactly what Annalise did right before talking to Sam.

That's right! And not only did she take off her wig and makeup, they then showed her putting on cocoa butter before the interaction. Damn! If the show's producers had shown her in the kitchen turning on the stovetop to medium heat and putting a hot comb through the hair of some neighborhood children, I would have fainted. It's not an overstatement when I write that watching a part of the black woman's beauty routine reflected back at me made me praise dance the way I do when I'm in the Pillsbury crescent-roll section of my grocery store. This scene was so real, so honest, so raw, so *everything* because *this* is what a lot of black women look like when not in public. To present that to America was huge. Not only did it show what beauty preparation is like for many black women, it let most, if not all, non-black people into a world that had previously been off-limits to them. Usually, the media has shown black women as resilient and unbelievably strong in the face of crisis, so for a show to reveal a BW's vulnerability is monumental. This scene, and in particular the wig removal, illustrated that black women do have emotions, do get hurt, and do express themselves. To have this happen on an extremely popular nighttime show on ABC was incredible. It made me die, go to heaven, say "wait a minute," and come back down to Earth the way you come back to your house when you realize you left the bathroom light on, because I needed to be alive to see how else Viola Davis is going to recontextualize black women for the rest of the world. And that, ladies and gents, is why Viola Davis's wig removal on *How to Get Away with Murder* is THE SINGLE GREATEST MOMENT IN BLACK WOMEN TELEVISION HISTORY.

Well, there you have it. This concludes your CliffsNotes guide to all the notable moments in black hair history. Surely, I left some of your favorites out, and for that, I'm only half-sorry. To be honest, you're lucky you got this much from me. This essay was originally going to be nothing but a series of photos of me kneeling before a Solange Knowles shrine I built for her (which is just images of all her various hairstyles, Lawry's seasoning salt, shea butter lotion, a piece of weave I found off the street because Solange likes "found art," and flakes from my ashy kneecap as a sacrifice), but then my editor was like, "That's ignorant." To which I responded, "Good. Point." So here we are, friends, with a list that will remind us all to celebrate black hair and black beauty no matter how it's presented. Now, if you'll excuse me, I'm going to go be busy *not* dismantling my Solange shrine I *didn't* build. *Heh.*

My Nine Favorite
Not-So-Guilty Pleasures

I've never liked people labeling certain things I enjoy as a "guilty pleasure" because it's usually code for "Phoebe doing 'white-people shit.'" OK, fine. That assessment may be a skosh valid when I'm playing boccie or going to a Billy Joel concert. But somehow that phrase now includes me buying sliced fruit and attending the doctor regularly. That's not me doing "white people shit." That's just me "living my best life shit."

Generally, *guilty pleasure* describes run-of-the-mill activities such as reading gossip blogs, putting whipped cream on a latte, and crashing a real estate open house with—*gasp!*—no intention of buying a house but all the intentions of eating the free cookies. Sorry not sorry, but none of these count as guilty pleasures, and since I went to a Catholic high school, I ought to know. Guilt is what a guy feels when he's on the dance floor and realizes that his boner has gone rogue and is banging against his classmate's back as if he's a cruise-ship musician during a steel drum solo. Liking a cheesy '80s movie? Not so much. At least not for me. I like what I like. No guilt to be found here. No sirree, Bob. In fact, I think we ought to come up with a better term than *guilty pleasure*.

How about *Your Life Is One Big Bowl of "Oy Vey." Here's Why*. Not bad for a first pass, but we can do better. *You Is a Damn Fool. Here Are Exhibits A–P to Illustrate Why*. Hmm, closer. *Things You Are Strangely Proud of Liking Even Though They Clearly Prove You're Kind of a Hot Sloppy Joe Mess*. Hmm, doesn't quite roll off the tongue, does it? Guess we're stuck with *guilty pleasure*, but please note that I don't feel sheepish about anything that follows below. Without further ado, here are my nine favorites:

Not-So-Guilty Pleasure #1:
Ranking Members of U2 in the Order of Whom I Want to Sleep With

I, Phoebe Robinson, am a U2-aholic. As of writing this, I'm in my seventeenth year as a fan. I once saw them thrice at Madison Square Garden in the span of eight days, and I wore a kiss me, i'm irish T-shirt to try to get their attention. It did not work, but the offer still stands, fellas. Anyway, being a superfan means I think *and* talk about them often. Whenever I meet someone new, I often present them with this deep philosophical conundrum: Rank in order from first to last choice the members of U2 you would sleep with and why. This, of course, is asked only so I can reveal who I would sleep with and, naturally, I pretend as though this is the first time I ever thought about it. This may seem strange on my part, but I feel like you really get to know a person this way, as opposed to asking the standard "What would you do if you had a time machine?" Kill Hitler? So clichéd! News flash: One cannot simply walk up to Adolf Hitler and take him like he is a steamed dumpling sample from Costco. More important, hypothetically killing Hitler tells me nothing about who I'm talking to other than that the person is not a sociopath. Now, ranking the members of U2 as potential sexual partners? I'll learn everything about him or her that I need to know. So where do I stand with the boys of U2? Glad you asked:

1. **The Edge, Lead Guitarist**

   OK, sure he's a great guitarist, songwriter, and backup vocalist for Bono, *blah, blah, blah*. Those things originally had him at number three on this list, but he skyrocketed straight to the top because at one of the concerts I attended last year, he winked at me in front my then-boyfriend. Please note that The Edge's eye foreplay was not the cause of the breakup. I mean, c'mon, give me a little credit here. This isn't some Jane Austen novel where stolen glances across a crowded room are enough to ignite a romance. However, I'm a straight girl, and a rock star winking at you is classic straight-girl catnip whether she is betrothed or not. So even though I didn't go to the bone zone with The Edge, I at least window-shopped there and said, "Hello, lovah," like Carrie Bradshaw used to say to shoes all the time on *Sex and the City*.

Now, I'm sure some of you are like, "Yeah, but what about those knit caps, tho? He's always wearing some sort of hat to cover his baldness." Annnnnnnnd? I'm always wearing some sort of padded bra to hide the fact I'm a 32A. The point is that The Edge and I both have some insecurities about our bodies, which bonds us like wig glue does a wig to Beyoncé's scalp. And when you're that deeply bonded, the sex will be bomb.com.

2. Bono, Lead Singer

His singing voice is angelic, powerful, and raw. His speaking voice is that of a sexy Irish god. When he opens his mouth, I start behaving like an old black church lady, which means I fan myself and pass around a collection plate, except instead of money, I'm putting my vajeen in it. But his voice is not the only reason I want to get down with him. He's philanthropic (through his RED campaign, he's helping to fund AIDS research), he's all about commitment (he's been with the band and his wife for over thirty years), but above all, he's physically attainable, or as it was described in 2015, homeboy has a "DadBod." No one tells you this, but when you enter your thirties, you will find vaguely in-shape bodies ridiculously attractive as opposed to your Chris Hemsworth predilections of the past. This is not to say that ripped dudes turn you off. It's just that the DadBod signifies comfort—in one's skin, in throwing a middle finger to vanity, and in eating what *tastes* good as opposed to what makes one look good—and for me, comfort equals home. DadBod is a home that smells like cinnamon and plush carpeting that you can massage your toes in. Seeing a dude be that chill in his own skin makes me want to get turned out like a reversible white-water rafting jacket from Eddie Bauer (aka get laid a lot).

3. **Adam Clayton, Bassist**

Y'all, I'm just going to be really real here. Adam is next because he dated Naomi Campbell. She's black; I'm black. So there's no way I'm getting rejected. Right? OK, there's one *teensy tiny* difference between Ms. Campbell and me. She's a supermodel. I, on the other hand, am a supermodel in the way that a McDonald's salad is a salad. And much like that bowl of Mickey D's wet lettuce and tomato slices, you'll settle for it, but you're not going to post a picture of it on Instagram. The point is that Adam is clearly down with the brown (that sounded way cooler in my head), so he can do as the great Billy Ocean once instructed and "Get outta my dreams, get into my California king with Target bedding." J/K. It's a queen. J/K, the sequel, I live in NYC; I have a full-sized bed. Doy.

4. **Larry Mullen Jr., Drummer**
   Yes, his modelesque jawline is gorgeous and sharp enough to grate a wedge of Parmesan. Sure, he's got biceps and triceps for days. Of course, being incredibly talented at banging on drums all day means that he is most likely to put his thing down, flip it, and reverse it. But his name is Larry. Y'all. I can't call out "Larry" during sex. I'm not about that life.

Not-So-Guilty Pleasure #2:
Traveling with a Suitcase Full of Dirty Clothes So I Can Do Laundry for Free at My Parents' House

My New York City apartment is old and overpriced, and my upstairs neighbor blasts Luther Vandross because, I guess, it's easier and less invasive then spraying Jheri curl juice all over my bedroom walls. My home's biggest flaw, though, is that it's too small to have a washer/dryer. Right now you might be thinking, *Hey, Pheebs, that's not much of a sacrifice; you could live in any of the other forty-nine states in America and have a washer/dryer*. LOL. Eighty-three percent of the reason people stay in NYC is that the city has seduced us by negging us like a dude trying to pick up a woman who is way out of his league. I know I'm great; the city knows I'm great, but it doesn't give a damn, which makes me go, "Maybe I'm not?" and therefore I sometimes put up with going to a neighborhood Laundromat that smells like meat pies left on a window ledge.

If the only issue here was that the Laundromat stunk, I could put up with it. But there are other annoyances that add up that allow me to justify flying dirty underwear halfway across the country. First of all, there's the logistics of *getting* to the Laundromat, which involves schlepping heavy rolls of quarters in my purse. Listen, I already have cocoa butter in my bag—and not just one safe-for-airplane-travel-sized bottle. I have *three*. That may seem like a lot, but I like having enough lotion on hand to moisturize all black people within a hundred-foot radius. Just think of me as a Wi-Fi hotspot for ashy knees and elbows. Plus, whenever I arrive, without fail, half the washers are out of order, meaning that I have to fight over the available ones with OBLs, aka old black ladies, who always give me that "You know, the arches in my feet sure are tired from marching for your rights" look. I can't compete with that. So they win the washers, and I have to wait my turn.

During this waiting period, I have a bevy of options to help pass the time. I can watch whatever is on TV in the Laundromat, which is typically something from the latter half of Diane Keaton's oeuvre, where she's having an orgasm for the first time since Ford was shot, or she's trying to encourage Rachel McAdams and Sarah Jessica Parker to hug it out over tuna casserole. If I'm not in the mood for a movie, I can always read a book, judge other people's kids who are running around like they're at a Chuck E. Cheese's, or do my all-time favorite thing: avoid eye contact with strange dudes who read somewhere that they should go to unexpected places like the library, grocery store, and you guessed it, the Laundromat to pick up women. Men of the world, stop this. Women need a break from horny dudes charging at them like soldiers in *Braveheart*. Please let us sort through our dirty clothes in peace without worrying about you trying to get a sneak at my *Blue's Clues* underoos. (Please tell me I'm not the only grown-ass woman still buying cartoon undies for funsies.) And while significantly less annoying than the dudes that hit on you, it's worth noting that there's also always an assortment of people of color wandering into the 'mat, selling bootleg DVDs. I want to be like, "You know United Colors of Benetton exists, right? Go model, you cinnamon angel. Or be a jazz musician down at the bayou. Whatever. Just save yourself!" But I say nothing and they continue to be pushy about moving product. I gotta tell you, it's really difficult to refuse purchasing *Snow Dogs* for moral reasons while sorting knock-off Lululemon yoga pants into piles.

Anyway, the wait eventually ends, and I finally get to use the washers. Then it's on to the dryers. I have a theory about them. Remember in *The Dark Knight* when Alfred (played by Michael Caine) tells Bruce Wayne (Christian Bale) that "some men just want to watch the world burn"? Those men are definitely the ones who designed Laundromat dryers, which is a very specific breed of the devil. These dryers either dry clothes until they're scalding hot like a Golden Corral fondue fountain *or* they leave them damp like a men's bathroom sink. As you can see, I simply have no recourse but to rack up frequent flyer miles transporting dirty clothes across the country. I don't know about your parental units, but mine really have it together when it comes to laundry. They have it together in many other ways, such as having a fully stocked fridge at all times—and not just with the basics, like bread, milk, and eggs. I'm talking about luxury spices that you might only see in a wicker basket on *Chopped*, vegan food items that Oprah has endorsed, and enough produce to make a fresh summer salad whenever the mood strikes. Just like when Honey Boo Boo said everyone is a little bit gay, it seems like every parent is a little bit Gwyneth Paltrow: the Goop Years after the kids leave the house. And Ma and Pa Robinson are no exception.

My parents have an entire room dedicated to the sorting, washing, drying, and folding of laundry, and the place smells like dryer sheets and childhood. When running, the washer lets out a steady hum that says, "When I'm done with your clothes, you'll be singing: 'Ain't nobody dope as me / I'm dressed so fresh so clean.'" You guys, this washer is *peak* Outkast. As for the dryer? Perfecto. If a person were to play it in a movie— don't ask me why—it would be played by Meryl Streep. The dryer is that damn good.

The pièce de résistance? Doing laundry at my parents' house is *free*. That's means no lugging around heavy bags of quarters that put me in full-on Paul Robeson "Nobody Knows the Trouble I've Seen" Negro spiritual mode. Who wouldn't be thrilled about that?

Not-So-Guilty Pleasure #3:
Pretending I'm a Celebrity Whose Husband Has Just Passed Away and I'm Doing an Interview on *60 Minutes* about How I'm Overcoming the Tragedy

And yes, I know this make me nonbiodegradable garbage. If I were biodegradable garbage, we could at least turn me into mulch and use it to grow cilantro that would eventually end up as garnish in a bowl of guacamole. Unfortunately, I am merely a musty boot found at the bottom of the river.

Not-So-Guilty Pleasure #4:
Watching Fan-Made YouTube Videos about Fictional TV/Movie Couples

In a lot of ways, there are no better love stories than scripted Hollywood ones. Bridget Jones and Mark Darcy? Yes, please. Jerry Maguire and Dorothy Boyd? Tugging on my heartstrings. Joe Manganiello and that Aquafina bottle of water he hit from the back in *Magic Mike XXL*? Someone let me know where this couple is registered because I will buy them all of the Cuisinart appliances.

But what's even better than these love stories are fan-made videos that take the histories of entire relationships and boil them down to their essence in five minutes or less so that viewers can relive all the cute, swoon-worthy moments over and over again. Snippets of superwitty and high-level banter that means, "Hey, I kinda like you, too." The moment when a guy realizes the woman he's with is naturally beautiful as she's eating a messy burger and getting ketchup on her face. The palpable sexual tension while a woman ties a man's tie for him. (One quick thing about that. How does a female character, who we can practically guarantee has never worn a tie before because Hollywood can't fathom a woman playing with gender aesthetics while also being desirable to the opposite sex, all of a sudden have the expert tie-knotting skills of a dandy?) Much like a *Now That's What I Call Music!* compilation album, each of these situations represents the "best of" these relationships. That "Remember when" nostalgia is something that I yearn for as I get older and, if I'm being a little honest, a little more cynical.

So for me, fan-made YouTube videos, in all their lo-fi glory, are my "break glass in case of emergency" for my unpredictable love life. They inspire me, remind and encourage me to be a hopeless romantic sometimes, and prove that I will watch anything in 480i quality if there is the promise of a kiss scored by Adele at the end. So thank you, oats4sparkle. Your Josh Lyman–Donna Moss/*The West Wing* vids got me through all of 2009, all of 2010, and most of 2011. Or as I like to call those years, "The Drought That Was So Bad It Could've Been the Inciting Incident in *Chinatown*."

Not-So-Guilty Pleasure #5:
Googling Myself

As a stand-up comic, TV writer, and occasional actress, I could easily pretend I Google myself as industry research, but I'd be lying. When my career is in a state of inertia, I look up positive reviews either to confirm that I've chosen the correct profession or to just bask in the glow of a recent triumph. Either way, the goal is to maintain drunk-girl-wearing-a-pushup-bra-on-a-reality-TV-show level of confidence at all times, and Googling myself is a hell of a lot cheaper than a Victoria's Secret bra and Jose Cuervo.

Now, I know most people will never, *ever* own up to Googling themselves. I'm guessing that's because turning the Internet into an old librarian thumbing through the Dewey Decimal System of any and all things YOU is considered shamefully self-absorbed behavior. Well, I hate to be the bearer of bad news, but we're all Narcissus and we fell into the river long ago. Might as well add Googling yourself to the vanity pile, which includes writing boring information on Facebook and then refreshing the web browser every ten minutes to see if there is an uptick in "likes," or posting selfies on Instagram just to have a someone on the web say that he ~~thinks you're beautiful~~ wants to fuck your face and then have you make him a sandwich.

For me, Googling myself can be a form of quality

control. Friends and family, for the most part, won't tell you the truth, but for whatever reason, strangers will lay it out for you, albeit unfiltered and often unsolicited. This truth can make you laugh, or make you sad, or happy, or furious, but I think, ultimately, it can also be beneficial if you do it right. I'll give you an example.

Years ago, I did Boston's Women in Comedy Festival, and one of my stand-up sets was recorded and put online. The feedback was mostly complimentary, but one person wrote, "Hello, armpit stains." I scrolled back up to the video and there they were: two circles of sweat the size of coasters. UGH. Listen, I'm a sweaty person; I always have been. But I had managed to keep it under control with aluminum-based deodorants until the fear of getting Alzheimer's made me switch to Tom's of Maine. People had warned me that Tom's might not be strong enough for me, but I shrugged them off and asked Jesus to take the wheel. Here's the thing about asking Jesus to take the wheel: Sometimes he doesn't and instead lets you crash your Toyota Corolla into a tree. To put it more plainly, Tom's didn't work at all, and I ended up smelling like a dirty river person who has more dreadlocks than teeth. And apparently, everyone on the Internet could now see that. I immediately went back to using antiperspirant, and I have that anonymous commenter to thank, because a friend, if they are worth their salt, will never tell you when your body embarrasses you. Thankfully, a stranger will. So I recommend that everyone who can emotionally handle it to Google themselves. However, there are rules you must abide by in order to not end up as sad as those polar bears floating on melting icecaps in World Wildlife Fund commercials:

- **Reading YouTube Comments about Yourself Is Absolutely Banned.**

  I refuse to let you take into consideration anything YouTube commenters write about you, when 90 percent of them are like, "Since you just watched Beyoncé's 'Countdown' video, let me tell about *all* of my 9/11 conspiracy theories." There is nothing useful for you here.

- **The Time You Spend Googling Yourself Cannot Be Longer Than an Episode of *The Big Bang Theory*.**

  Only a monster spends hours looking themselves up online. Don't be disgusting.

- **Never Ever Respond to a Troll.**

  There's a difference between someone trying to engage in conversation with or about you and someone whose sole purpose is to seek and destroy you. That difference is the dialogue quickly devolves into "dat article suked. ur fat n ugly. ur mom won't stop callin me after i left her suk me off last nite." You don't need that.

■ **If Someone Has Taken an Amazing Picture of You, Immediately Make It Your Profile Picture.**

Sometimes you'll be at party, event, or a performance and a photographer will take a photo of you that will make you look like Solange, Gisele Bündchen, and Lupita Nyong'o combined. And you will think, *I could totally have sex with myself right now*. You are correct. Go do that and then when you're done, send that photographer an Edible Arrangement as a thank-you ASAP.

■ **No Matter What Is Written about You—Good or Bad—Don't Let It Go to Your Head.**

Public opinion, like stock on the Dow Jones, often fluctuates. Take none of it to heart except if it comes from a person whom you love. And even then, you kind of have to take it easy on how much loved ones influence your self-perception. If you allow yourself to absorb too much of the positivity, you'll think your shit don't stink, and that's how the world ended up with Rebecca Black's "Friday." On the flip side, if you take the negative things they say

about you too much to heart, you and your
family/ friends will end up on an episode of
Dr. Phil. And trust me, you don't want to be
taking life advice from someone who is basically the by-product of a Popeyes commercial
and a Lyft mustache.

Not-So-Guilty Pleasure #6:
Having Pretend Subway Boyfriends

He's the dreamboat of the day on a crowded subway
train, who's seated across from me, reading a book. He
looks up, we lock eyes, and then he returns to his book. I,
on the other hand, have decided it. Is. On. We are dating
until the end of the commute.

There's beauty in having a subway boyfriend. I
started dating late in life, and I'm not particularly stellar
at it. I'm either in a relationship or very single because
flings are not my thing, so these flights of fantasy allow
me to envision drastically different lives than the one I
currently lead. Here's an example of how one of these
romances will play out. At the beginning of the trip,
this SB and I have sufficiently "meet-cuted": I get up to
look at the subway map, which is above his head, the
train jerks, I fall into his lap, knocking his Kindle to the
floor. I apologize; he asks me out. We have sex after five
dates, and we survive the dreaded DTR (define the relationship) talk. We are official boo thangs. By the time

we're going over the Manhattan Bridge and into the city, Subway Boyfriend and I have fully established inside jokes, met each other's parents, and gone on vacation to Turks and Caicos, Paris, and Charleston, South Carolina. Out of pride, he even teared up when I was nominated for a Golden Globe. But uh-oh. I'm three stops away from my destination. Time to cue up some Coldplay and end this relationship. We cry, fight, plead with each other that maybe we should give it another chance. But we know it wouldn't work, so we deal with the gut-wrenching task of dividing the items we bought when we moved in together, deciding who gets custody of our favorite tapas restaurant, and making the empty promise that we'll be friends. And as this breakup montage plays in my mind while Chris Martin sings, "When you try your best, but you don't succeed," I go, "We did. We tried our very best." And this is my stop, Subway Boyfriend. I have to get off here and buy $50 worth of items at Walgreens to mask the fact that one of the items I'm buying is tampons. Godspeed, SB.

Not-So-Guilty Pleasure #7: WWE Wrestling

La-la-la, I can't hear you. Wrestling is real and perfect and a testament to sheer athleticism. Wrestling is real. La-la-la.

Not-So-Guilty Pleasure #8:
Ordering Enough Food from McDonald's for
Two People, but I Just Eat It All.

To be clear, it's not like I went to pick up food for a friend and on the way back home, I shoved it all in my dumb face in a Bruce Banner–esque blackout. This gluttony is a solo job, baby, and it usually occurs when I'm stressed. I don't care what anyone says; stress eating is amazing. Euphoric. Heavenly. Filling your body with carbs and beverages that aren't within the Crayola crayon color spectrum and then falling into a deep, drunk-like sleep the way a toddler does after hours of play is not the worst way to end an evening.

I'm not a self-destructive person—meaning no hard drugs, minimal alcohol, and zero dangerous physical activities—so eating fast food is my version of living on the edge. And it comes with relatively few consequences in the short term. I mean, freebasing cocaine on the regs will mess up your bank account, cause you to lose your friends, and lead to rehab, but eating comfort food that is terrible for you, will, OK, slowly kill you over many decades, but also like, maybe not? After all, I see tons of old-ass people getting McDonald's hash browns at 10:30 a.m.; I have yet to meet an octogenarian cutting up blow with their AARP card. My drug of choice—McDonald's (or In-N-Out Burger, if I'm in LA)—is clearly the superior one.

Now, if we're to believe the commercials airing on BET, all Mickey D establishments are full of black people singing R&B medleys about chicken nuggets. That couldn't be further from the truth. No matter which location I visit, the vibe is always "Yeah, I shouldn't be here. Don't tell my wife/dad/ son/guidance counselor," because everyone has seen the documentaries, heard the health reports, and eaten the kale chips that are supposed to be an equally delicious substitute for McD's addictive French fries (whoever started this rumor can die in a fire, thank you very much). And I'm not writing this as a kale basher. I was eating kale *way* before it went mainstream. Kale was my Black Eyed Peas before they added Fergie and sold out. I'm just saying that thin strips of potatoes deep-fried in oil laced with sugar taste infinitely better. I always start my ordering process at Mickey D's with a softball: a crispy chicken sandwich plus cheese. A newbie cashier will ask if I want cheddar or American, but the grizzled, "let's cut the shit" cashiers will straight up be like, "the yellow or white one," ruining all illusion that I was ever choosing anything that was in the cheese family. Those are the employees I like the most. They're not about pretense. They keep it raw and real, like Dr. Iyanla Vanzant, but instead of fixing lives of C-list black celebs, they're taking my order. Anyway, I start with the sandwich, then I add a large fry, and finally, a VitaminWater Zero because, no joke, that's when I decide, "Oooh, I need to be healthy real quick."

Guys. I know. You're either healthy or you're not and I, the not-so-proud occasional consumer of McDonald's, am legit flirting with unhealthy like he's a basic-ass dude on *The Bachelor*. And the flirting often turns into a full-court press offensive because I'll usually add to the order by tossing a ten-piece nugget into the mix.

What I love about this is that it forces the cashier to give me the once-over. In weaker moments, I'll check my phone and mumble, "I'm pretty sure my boyfriend wanted the ten-piece. Lemme double-check." But when I'm feeling bold and defiant, I match the cashier's stare with one of my own that says, "Yeah, if the mountain won't come to Muhammad, then Muhammad must go to the mountain." In this case, I'm Muhammad and the mountain is the diabeetus that Wilford Brimley warned us about in those Liberty Medical commercials. Having recognized that I'm the superior opponent, the cashier backs down, gives me a head nod that probably means, "You won this time. But let's be honest, did you really? Look at what you're doing to yourself." I acknowledge the head nod with one of my own that says, "You called cheese 'the yellow one.' So if anything, we'll be conference calling Iyanla together, alright?"

Not-So-Guilty Pleasure #9:
Sidewalk Rage

Remember that Chris Rock bit where he said you haven't truly been in love unless you've imagined how you would kill your significant other? I feel the same about being a New Yorker. Some say that if you weren't lucky enough to be born here, you become a New Yorker after being a resident for ten years. They're wrong. If you're a nonnative, you become a New Yorker when your sidewalk rage is so strong that you feel the need to murder. Instances that trigger sidewalk rage:

- People walking too slowly in front of you.

- People walking too closely behind you.

- People having a moment of hesitation because they aren't sure they're headed in the correct direction, so they slow down for a brief moment.

- People who are not you and are on the sidewalk at the same time as you.

I'm mostly being facetious, but there is also a small part of me that does believe that this rage is rational and legitimate. Walking is an integral part of the NYC experience: New Yorkers walk to mass transportation, to work, to bodegas (aka mini convenience stores) that stay open way too late just because they've decided that 2 a.m. seems like an appropriate time to eat Little Debbie snacks. (It's not, and I'm sure someone has already written a think piece about how having any and every craving that caters to every human desire available constantly is emblematic of the "iGeneration," but I digress.) The point is that New Yorkers have lots of places to be and we have to get to each and all of them very quickly. Why? While there isn't an official pamphlet that states the cause for the constant urgency, I think it has something to do with the fact that New York is the city of the multihyphenate.

What do I mean by that? Everyone I know here is a nanny–singer–WebMD doctor–cat whisperer–actor– paralegal– bartender hybrid. To make it in New York, you need seventeen jobs. There are the ones that pay the bills but you're unqualified for, like when I was an entertainment lawyer's assistant for four years when the only legal training I had was watching *Ally McBeal*. Then there are the gigs that put you on the path toward achieving your dreams, but the pay is shit. Case in point: One time, my compensation for doing a stand-up show was a vibrator with a computer-USB-cord charger, which I have refused to use till this day because I'm pretty sure a vibe teaming up with a laptop in order to power on is what *Terminator 3: Rise of the Machines* was warning us about. So as you can see, we New Yorkers spend the majority of our time working, which means we're also spending time getting to and from those jobs. Then we have to factor in time traveling to see friends, go on dates, and run errands in activewear—a category of clothing that is the biggest crime against humanity since Pol Pot—because all women in NYC from about the age of nineteen until forty-nine dress like they're on their way to compete in *American Ninja Warrior* yet only about 0.8 percent of us are in shape enough to actually compete on *American Ninja Warrior*.

Anyway, what I'm getting at here is that everyday New Yorkers are trying to accomplish more than what's possible in a twenty-four-hour day. The pressure is on, so the last thing we need is a heavy-footed stranger moseying along in front of us like he's sweater shopping in the mall while listening to Train's "Hey, Soul Sister." That kind of mess is likely to make me want to shank him. And yes, my default setting for sidewalk rage is "shank a bitch," but it wasn't always this way. That kind of anger is only achieved by living in the Big Apple for a long time. In case you're wondering where you fall on the scale, it's time I break out the different kinds of side-walk rage that lead one up to being a full-on New Yorker:

Letting out a passive-aggressive sigh that lets the person in front of you know that they are walking a little bit slower than you like, but it's no big deal because no one's perfect and besides, it's pretty nice outside. *Ooh, there's a plastic bag floating in the wind. Very* American Beauty, you think, *God, this city is amaz*—Yep, a stranger just shoved past you because *you* slowed down.— **WELCOME TO NEW YORK, NOW GET THE HELL OUTTA MY WAY.**

Blurting out "Un-fucking-believable" at a couple strolling along, holding hands, so you have to walk around them. Now in front of the lovebirds, you turn back around and yell, "Ya won't last!"—**HAPPY FIVE-YEAR ANNIVERSARY OF LIVING IN BROOKLYN!**

Mentally plotting to become friends with attorney Gloria Allred for several years. Key parts of plan include brunch dates, sharing secrets, and attending her daughter's christening. All of this is necessary because the next time a group of European tourists comes to an abrupt stop in the middle of the sidewalk that makes you change direction by a few degrees, they will breed a fury so irrational that you're willing to murder this Euro family. And when you're done, you'll call Gloria and go, "Girl, it happened and I need your help."—**ULTIMATE NEW YORKER.**

Having lived here for fourteen years, I definitely fall into the last category. I'm aware that getting my blood pressure up like that serves no purpose, but I love it. Getting pissed that someone is slowing me down—*don't they know I have somewhere to be?!*—instead of getting mad at myself for not leaving home ten minutes earlier is not only ridiculous but also very New York. We're always running behind, over-booked, and missing the train all because some idiot (*not* us) made us late. "You gotta be frickin' kidding me," we'll say to ourselves. Then when we meet up with the person who has been waiting for us, we'll relay the story of a moron (again, never us) who is the cause for our tardiness. This "you gotta be frickin' kiddin' me" vibe followed by total lack of culpability is so quintessential New York, and anytime I do that, I feel like I belong.

Wow, I can't believe I shared with you my game plan of befriending Gloria Allred just on the off chance I murderize a European family who's en route to see *Hamilton*. To be clear, the disbelief is not because I feel bad about this fantasy—'memba this is a guilt- (and judgment-) free zone—it's just that I didn't realize we had gotten so close already. I guess that was bound to happen after I shared some of my "not-guilty guilty pleasures." Truth is it's kind of hard to stay acquaintances after I just told you that I'd voluntarily sleep with four fifty-plus-year-old white dudes. I mean, there's no coming back from that, so I suppose the only thing to do is accept that this revelation is all a part of my journey and a part of who I am. And so are all the other things that made the cut on my "guilty pleasures" list. I'm not going to feel weird or embarrassed about them and neither should you about the things you love. Make it known that you like some occasionally bizarre shit because…

so does everyone! News flash, we all like some occasionally bizarre shit because we *are* occasionally bizarre people. And that bizarre shit that we like is a reflection of us, so to feel guilty about those things is basically like feeling guilty about a part of ourselves. Screw. That. Let that freak flag fly, baby! Let's stop apologizing for every kooky, random, left-of-center thing that melts our butter. Let's own up to all the things we love and move the fuck on dot org. And when I say, "let's," that includes you, dear reader. Yeah, no. Don't look at the person next to you. I'm talking to YOU. We're all in this together, right? Great, because I just showed you my freak flag. Now show me yours.

Welcome to Being Black

In every black person's life, there's a moment when they go from believing their blackness merely serves as another descriptor, like "she has a slight overbite" or "he snorts when he laughs," to their blackness and all the complications surrounding that identity becoming the number one thing that defines them. Remember in *The Amazing Spider-Man* when Uncle Ben told Peter Parker, "With great power comes great responsibility"? And then Parker turned into Spider-Man and went on to be celebrated by society for his heroism? Well, realizing you're black is exactly like that, except in the place of special powers, an uncle who is mad chill about your newfound special powers, and everybody high-fiving your awesomeness, there's the following: coming to terms with being treated like the "Other," accepting that a lot of people will view your actions as either defying or affirming preconceived notions about you, and figuring out ninjalike ways to escape the circle coworkers randomly form around you and another black person because they're hoping a dance battle will pop off.

To be fair, these kinds of adjustments happen with every race, every sexual orientation, and any group that does not fall into the category of "straight white dude." However, because of the centuries-long antiblack sentiment in America, it seems that some want to assign particular characteristics to blackness as a means of flattening or dehumanizing people. Blackness is not a monolith. There's nerdy black, jock black, manic pixie dream black, sassy black, shy black, conscious black, hipster black... the list goes on and on. But some people don't want to believe that, because if varying degrees of blackness become normalized, then that means society has to rethink how they treat black people. In other words, if you allow black people to be as complicated and multidimensional as white people, then it's hard to view them as the Other with all the messy pejorative, stereotypical, and shallow ideas that have been assigned to that Otherness.

And it can't be understated that these ideas become internalized, no matter how hard you fight them. As a result of these negative labels, for example, I and other people wind up adjusting our behaviors to counter the negative stereotypes or to avoid becoming the butt of jokes. I'll overtip to combat the stereotype that black people don't tip well. Most, if not all, of my black friends have been mocked for speaking intelligently, yet if their diction were poor, they would have been dinged for that. Damned if you do, damned if you don't, as they say. In my apartment, I'm more hesitant to blast Missy

Elliott than Sting for fear of my neighbors being like, "Of course, the black girl is playing hip-hop loudly like she's on the set of *Breakin' 2: Electric Boogaloo*." So the peeps in 4A, that's why you hear "Fields of Gold" on the damn repeat. Sowwie! Anyway, the point is this type of hyper-awareness is taxing.

Given that it's such an important aspect of a POC's identity, it's interesting to me that I can't remember the first time I ever realized I was black, in the sense of how the world viewed me. Normally, I would chalk up this blank space in my memory bank to nothing more than getting older, except there are other, slightly less life-defining things that I remember to a T. Like that time when I tastefully explained what the X-rated term *hummer* meant during dinner with my ex-boyfriend's family, and somehow ended up charming everyone in the process. Seriously, I was breaking down a randy sex act to his family, and I was like "Jennifer Lawrence falling up the stairs at the 2013 Oscars" charming. I remember that moment so well, but the moment I truly realized I was black? I got bupkis. There was no aha moment, no "Ohhhhhhhhh, I see. The game. Done. Changed. For. Me. Moment." Maybe because I'm a child of the '90s, which was a much better decade to be black than the '40s, '50s, or '60s, which were eras where the racism was so palpable that the moment when blacks recognized they were viewed as the Other would be firmly etched in their minds forever. Not that racism didn't exist in the '90s—hello, Rodney King!—it's just that the kind of racism I might have been exposed to was less Little Rock Nine and more "after-school special where everyone learns a lesson." So since I can't remember when I realized that everything was changing, the next best thing is to recall the most recent time I was reminded I'm black. And like any story about funky behavior due to race, the setting for this tale is... a Michaels craft store in Manhattan.

A little background: Michaels is where I go when I'm feeling like Martha Stewart, but my bank account is more like French Stewart. #NoShade. I mean, I love me some *3rd Rock from the Sun*, but that show ended more than fifteen years ago, and I'm sure all of French's residuals from acting on *3rd* are gone by now. Anyway, Michaels is where I go to get my arts-and-crafts fix and say phrases like "this really ties a room together" and "I'm not so sure this fits my design aesthetic." You guys, it took me two months to unpack two U-Haul boxes in my apartment because watching TV is more interesting to me than finding a place for books I've bought to look smart in front of my houseguests but haven't read yet (here's looking at you, William Faulkner oeuvre that Oprah nominated as a Book Club selection in 2005). Safe to say, my design aesthetic is "lazy as fuck." Nevertheless, I'm an interior designer at heart, so armed with decoration knowledge I acquired from TLC and HGTV, I walk the aisles of Michaels, imagining how I'm going to "transform my living space," which mostly means throwing up some wall art.

As much as I love interior design, framing is not a lifelong passion of mine. In fact, I didn't get into framing until I turned thirty years old. Wow, I think I just unlocked the key to drying out your own vagina like a negligee on a clothesline. Just utter the phrase "I didn't get into framing until…" and poof! Bone dry. Anyway, I've grown to love framing, which seemed to happen right around the time I started doing things worth framing. Not that I didn't achieve anything in my twenties, but it's all ordinary stuff, like "I didn't go home with weird guy at bar and instead went home and watched a movie alone" and "my paycheck direct deposited at the same time my rent check cleared." These are the sorts of things that say, "Yeah, you're an adult… but you're not a *real* adult until you do your laundry before you run out of underwear." I am slowly morphing into the latter kind of adult, and part of that process means I now frame things instead of duct-taping them to the wall. The most recent thing I wanted to trick out was a *New York Times* profile that was written about the stand-up/storytelling podcast show *2 Dope Queens* that my work wife, Jessica Williams, and I do for WNYC. This article, which ended up on the front page of the Arts section, is hands-down one of the coolest and most surreal moments of my career. I felt like I was being baptized in Oprah's titty sweat, which I believe is how you know for certain something should be framed.

So I ordered the frame job from Michaels and went to pick it up a few weeks later. It was shortly before Christmas, but the framing department was practically empty, save for two employees, one white and the other racially ambiguous, or as it's called in the biz: Liberal Arts College Pamphlet Face. They were tapping away at their computers at the counter, seemingly just going through the motions of a typical workday; meanwhile, I was excited because I was about to see my career achievement in a frame. I approached them all smiles… and, nothing. No acknowledgment. Under normal circumstances, that would be ominous, but since this happened in NYC, the rudeness is standard-issue. A few minutes passed, though, and both employees had walked past me multiple times to get printouts, frame parts, etc., and had still failed to address me. I was slightly annoyed by that point, but I was on that "new year, new me" ish early, meaning I stopped approaching life as though my finger was on speed dial to Al Sharpton. This is not to say I had been wrong in those previous instances; I wasn't. However, constantly being on guard for racism can make one age in "old black people during the civil rights era" years. It's similar to aging in dog years except that you say, "Lord, I'm weary," all the time, and whenever you're at a wedding, you always ask the DJ to interrupt the dance party and put on a Nat King Cole slow jam. Anyway, despite my annoyance, I made sure to remain calm. *This is messed up. I know they see me. I'm a five-foot-seven black woman with a red weave,* I told myself, *but I'm going to rise abo—HOL'. UP.* A white lady wearing striped socks with wooden clogs—a style I normally think is incredibly stupid, but on her, looked hella cute—waltzed up to the counter and in less than ten seconds was helped by Liberal Arts College Pamphlet Face. I thought this was weird, but I tried to not take this personally, and I hoped that now the white employee would acknowledge me. She did not. Still, I said nothing because I wondered how long I was going to have to wait to get service. Turns out, quite a bit of time.

Several minutes pass. A white dude who looks like Justin Theroux minus the talent approaches, and the white lady employee damn near trips over her ovulation calendar to help him. She finishes with him and then goes and sits back down at her desk to, I don't know, answer casting calls for Yoplait commercials. In short, she is basic as fuck, and I'm STILL waiting. Finally, I go up to Yoplait Face and ask, "Can you please help me? Because I've been waiting ten minutes, and y'all refuse to see me?" She apologizes so quickly that I can tell she didn't hear my complaint at all. Her sorry was totally reflexive based off my displeased tone.

I wasn't happy with her nonapology, and so I tell her it was ridiculous that I had to wait so long. Yoplait Face apologized again, claiming that the delay was because it gets hectic during the holidays. Y'all. Y'ALL. The frames section at Michaels was barren as the convenience store in *I Am Legend*. I was the first customer to show up at the counter, so how did I end up being helped third? And why did she think I would fall for such a moronic lie? Like a Stepford wife, she wrapped my frame up, plastered a smile and vacant stare on her face, and said, "Happy holidays," as if she thought I was going to say it back to her. Like she expected me to do anything other than what I actually did, which was let her bullshit season's greetings hang in the air like Tom Cruise in *Mission: Impossible*.

Now, getting shitty customer service at the frames department in an arts-and-crafts store is pretty much the crux of #MiddleClassProblems, especially in comparison to how black people were treated fifty years ago. But just because this slight by the Michaels employee doesn't register high on the racism Richter scale doesn't mean it's something to ignore. Micro-aggressions like this accumulate over days, weeks, months, and they shape my experience as a black person. And this is not to say there aren't many wonderful things about being black. There are, and a lot of them have been absorbed by pop culture—fashion, music, food—but still, there are tons of things about being #TeamMelanin that blow.

Like how if I leave the race/ethnicity box empty on a site like Monster.com, I'll get more job inquiries from employers than if I were to check "black." Or how if I go apartment hunting solo, landlords tend to be ruder to me than if I bring a white friend along. Or those reminders that I'm not welcome to audition for casting calls via the following stipulations: "No braids, no twists, no dread-locks, only natural hair color allowed." Riiiiiight. Because the casting directors are totally going to turn away every brunette white actress who shows up with blond hair. All those things and many more reinforce the idea that *who I am* is the problem. And in the case of the Michaels incident, it seemed the universe was using this to say, "In case you forgot, I'm here to remind you. Welcome, once again, to being black."

There are many methods for coping with this reminder. Venting on social media and getting support from friends. Canceling dinner plans to spend the evening doing a Google image search of Michael B. Jordan. Daydreaming about having a white nanny who I put through a series of high-pressure "race tests" like "sing a pitch-perfect rendition of Stevie Wonder's version of the 'Happy Birthday' song" or "make sweet potato pie for my judgey-ass parents this Thanksgiving." You know, stuff that is fun for the whole family. But my personal favorite? Wishing that white people could, even for a day, experience both the subtle and not-so-subtle racism that black people (and all POCs) go through, just to understand how a lifetime of this kind of treatment changes you. And no, I don't mean pulling a C. Thomas Howell in the 1986 "comedy" *Soul Man*, which is a film so ludicrous, misguided, and racist in its attempt to show people what it's like to be black that when the KKK goes on retreats, they probably watch this on movie night. Seriously, *Soul Man is* just that bad. Wait… I can't just drop that reference and move along. Excuse me while we take a brief detour through this fuckery.

Here is the plot: CTH plays a rich kid named Mark, whose dad decides not to pay for his tuition *after* Mark has been accepted into Harvard Law School. So Mark comes up with the brilliant idea to *reapply* to Harvard Law as a "black" guy to get a scholarship that is for African-American students, so he ~~rubs a melted Hershey's bar all over his face~~ takes "tanning pills" to darken his skin and begins donning a curly wig. He lands the scholarship and assumes that life is going to be pretty easy as a black person because Cosby (cringe alert!) has a TV show. Ridiculous enough yet? Let's pause because I need to address a couple of things. One, it's *hilarious* that Mark thinks racism died because ONE black dude had a successful TV show. I guess Mark forgot it was the '80s, a decade in which black people spent 93 percent of their time going, "Hey, President Reagan, can you stop funneling cocaine into our neighborhoods?" But, sure, rich white kid, being black is totes a breeze. Secondly, I can't show up CPT (Colored People's Time) to Au Bon Pain and get breakfast at 11:30 a.m., but Mark can CPT his way into Harvard? LOL. Why is this movie acting like Harvard is a Sugar Ray concert in 2015 that you can show up to day-of and get a ticket?

So, Mark is living that black life on campus, which

is basically just him playing basketball and jive talkin' (shoot me in the face). Then he notices that people are mean to him because of the color of his skin! How mean? At one point, a white dude refers to him as a "black Negro," which sounds like an option on a US Census form from the 1890s but is supposed to be scathing. Are you kidding me??? C. Thomas Howell is wearing black-face for the majority of this film, and that's fine, but the movie's producers draw the line at a peripheral white character calling him "porch monkey" or "nigger"? I probably shouldn't write this, but I'm going to anyway: If you're going to be racist, which *Soul Man* certainly is, then you have to be INCLUSIVE with your racism. Don't pick and choose pieces of racism like it's IKEA furniture.

Anyway, shit gets real in *Soul Man* when Mark meets Sarah Walker, a black classmate and single mother who lost the scholarship to him and now must waitress to pay for her tuition. All of the sudden, Mark feels guilty—not because he took away money that could benefit a "real" black person, but because the black person he screwed over gives him a boner. Barf. Also, can we just comment about how absurd that Sarah is a waitress and she can afford to go to Harvard AND raise a child by herself AND also live in a world where nobody at Harvard treats her like trash for being a black single mom? As if that's not ridiculous enough, here comes the most unbelievable aspect of the movie: Sarah and Mark begin dating, and before long, she finds out the truth about him. Initially, she's mad, but she decides to forgive him and the two get back together by the end of the movie. And that, my friends, is how Mark finally learns that it's hard out there for black people. Right. Or he could have just, I don't know, asked a black person how hard life is. Or paid a black person $300 to teach a six-week Learning Annex course about what it's like to be black. Or read a book written by a black person. Or listen to the blues. There are so many options!

OK. Clearly, *Soul Man* is an over-the-top example of white people trying to comprehend the black experience. In reality, most people aren't taking extreme measures to learn. Some pick up knowledge when a case of police brutality becomes national news, or when they ask a black friend about his or her culture (i.e., "Pheebs, why are black people's dap handshakes more complicated than the Yankees' catcher signals to his pitcher?"). And still, there are other instances where some had no intentions of educating themselves but stumble into it, as was the case with Uniontown, Ohio, couple Jennifer Cramblett and Amanda Zinkon.

In 2011, these women decided to add to their family, so Cramblett was artificially inseminated at the Midwest Sperm Bank in hopes of getting the blond, blue-eyed baby of their dreams. Nine months later, the couple was in for a surprise: Their newborn daughter was biracial. There was a highly negligent mix-up at the sperm bank, and, as it turned out, Cramblett was impregnated with a black man's sperm. There's no denying that this clerical error was hugely inappropriate, but what follows is even worse. Three years later, Cramblett and Zinkon filed a wrongful birth and breach of warranty lawsuit against the sperm bank. Because this was such a unique case, the contents of the lawsuit got leaked to the public—and what's in there is cringeworthy:

> Getting a young daughter's haircut is not particularly stressful for most mothers, but to Jennifer, it is not a typical routine matter, because Payton has hair typical of an African-American girl. To get a decent cut, Jennifer must travel to a black neighborhood, far from where she lives, where she is obviously different in appearance, and not overtly welcome.

Memo to Jennifer and Amanda: There are hundreds of Tracee Ellis Ross–looking women on YouTube, moisturizing their biracial hair like they're putting an egg wash on a tray of hot cross buns. So watch those videos and apply that knowledge so your child's hair won't look like the lint filter in a Whirlpool dryer. Quit acting like you're merely *50 Shades of Concerned* over which grapeseed oil to use on her hair.

OK, fine. I am being a tad flippant here, but I do have a point. The Midwest Sperm Bank's mistake is inexcusable and their reaction (issuing an apology and offering a partial refund) doesn't make their mix-up any better, but when it comes down to it, what's done is done. Payton, Jennifer and Amanda's daughter, is a half-black living being in this world. Her parents making it *national knowledge* that she is not necessarily the child they envisioned and hiding that disappointment under the guise of "It's Hard Out There for People Who Are Darker Than a U-Haul Box" is cruel and unforgiving. Yes, life will be difficult for Payton, as it is for any POC, but the truth is her parents are making it harder for her. By denying their child in this way, Zinkon and Cramblett have inflicted irreparable psychological damage on their daughter that will forever shape her self-perception—a self-perception that already has to contend with the litany of negative outside forces that affect the lives of every POC.

What I am about to write may seem like a sweeping generalization to anyone who is not a person of color in this country, but here goes: For POCs, having a strong sense of self often feels like a Sisyphean task. Every. Single. Day. This is not to imply that white people don't struggle; of course they do. Yet, there is no denying that whiteness being "The Standard" makes everything a little bit simpler for them. Think about this. According to the 2009 American Community Survey, Brooklyn is 54.6 percent white and 45.4 percent ethnic, yet in my neighborhood Walgreens, I have to go on an *Amazing Race*–esque journey just to find the products for my skin type. POCs are an afterthought if they're lucky, which explains why, for example, the makeup appropriate for my skin color in my Wally's is crammed into a corner like Christmas lights in an attic. To be fair, there *are* moments when POCs are not treated like the Other. In my experience, it's often the "Oh, Wow! You're Not Like My Racist Preconceptions of the Others, but You Also Aren't One of Us Either," which is as much of a compliment as doing the sign of the cross before drunken sexy-times is a form of birth control.

The truth is daily micro-aggressions like the ones mentioned above, as well as the macro ones, await someone like Payton. So instead of educating themselves about that, Cramblett and Zinkon forged ahead by suing for $50,000 for having, as their lawsuit claims, suffered "personal injuries, medical expense, pain, suffering, emotional distress, and other economic and noneconomic issues, and will do so in the future."

Pain. Suffering. Emotional distress. Oh, dear. Payton is going to grow up, use Google, and discover that her skin color and coarse hair were sources of duress for her parents. By Cramblett's own admission in the lawsuit, she lives in a racist neighborhood, but apparently that fact *only* became problematic when she found herself raising a biracial child. Sooo, if they had a white child, she would've been fine with raising him or her in a racist environment, perpetuating the same ignorance? This woman needs to sit down and study the "When White

112

Privilege Moonwalks Out of Your Life" pamphlet. Turns out it's a quick read because inside is just the following:

> People don't think you're white anymore. Say good-bye to the societal advantages that benefit whites in Western countries in a variety of social, political, or economic circumstances. Listen to N.W.A to cope, but when rapping along to them, don't say the N-word... because you are still white. Duh.

Hey, Jennifer and Amanda, are you now majorly inconvenienced on the smallest and biggest levels? Do you have to deal with people sometimes treating you like a Cheetos stain under their fingernail? Do you worry about your child's safety, as my parents did when my brother and I went into certain neighborhoods? Then WELCOME TO BEING BLACK. You don't get $50,000 because being a mother to a half-black child is hard. You swallow the indignities like I do when the color of my skin is explicitly why I don't get hired for certain jobs. You rise above the ugly statements—the *"Your natural hair isn't professional"* or *"You're black, but you're not black black"*—that are directed at you. You figure out how to live your best life because dammit, your mama and daddy love you. You tell yourself, "And still I rise," "I'm black, and I'm proud," "I'm young, gifted, and black," and then you go to bed, wake up, and do it all over again. Every. Single. Day. With no expectation of $50,000. With the understanding that forty acres and a mule is a dream that's been long deferred well before you were ever alive. You just live. That's what you do.

What you don't do is live in Uniontown, Ohio, for several years, give zero thought to the racism that happens there until your child's blackness becomes an earth-shattering inconvenience that undoes your decades of white privilege, and then turn on Pandora and play "Swing Low, Sweet Chariot" on repeat while crying crocodile tears. Please bottle those tears, package them in a self-addressed envelope, and mail them to:

Phoebe Robinson
c/o Haus of Fucks I Do Not Give
Anytown, USA 12345

Also, Jennifer, you don't go on NBC News as you did and say, "Payton will understand it wasn't about 'We didn't want you. We wanted a white baby'" when you and your girlfriend specifically requested white sperm the way I pick out a new weave for a Jamaican to put in my head. You wanted a white baby; pretending it's not about race is an insult to everyone's intelligence. Furthermore, to have the audacity to say, "She'll under-stand. It's all good," with the carefree attitude that I have when I put too much baking powder in cookie dough is horrifying.

But what's most important is the well-being of Payton. She will not understand why the fact that you ended up with a half-black baby made you cry on national television. Payton will not understand how until you had her, the importance of knowing anything about African-American history ranked somewhere below getting regular touch-ups on your Mark McGrath Sugar Ray frosted tips (#Callback), yet above... absolutely nothing. She's not going to understand why you feel entitled to $50,000 because you can't even last two years raising a half-black child without wanting to tap out as if Hulk Hogan put you in a headlock. She will not understand why, since you are apparently incapable of educating yourself about black culture and loving your child, you didn't give her up for adoption so she could potentially grow up in a much healthier environment. All she will understand is that *she was not wanted because of the color of her skin*.

But, at the very least, she will have the comfort of knowing that the legal system saw through your bullshit. DuPage County Judge Ronald Sutter threw your suit out because wrongful birth is usually for when medical testing was negligent and failed to show risks of congenital or hereditary disorders to a child before birth, not because your baby is not the race you wanted. You're lucky because if you two did get awarded that $50,000, then a charge of black people led by Octavia Velina Robinson and Phillip Martin Robinson Sr. (my parents) would've beat down upon the doors of the US Department of Treasury with the sheer force of a thousand thunderstorms and go, "Fuck you, pay me," like Paulie in *Goodfellas*.

So now that this lawsuit is done, you and your partner can turn your attention to the "less-than-ideal" situation: your child being black. So welcome. Take off your coats. You're going to be here a while, so please read this beginners' guide I give to all African-Americans when they enter the world.

Welcome to Being Black

Congratulations on being black! I know you had no choice in the matter, but I find that congratulating people on something, no matter what it is, just puts them in a fantastic mood, especially when you have to tell some bad news. Let's try it!

1. **You're Black. Here's a Lifetime Supply of Cocoa Butter! Now, Here's the Thing...**
   Yep, you're right. I didn't give you much time to enjoy the lotion. But it's because we have to get to the juicy stuff! Like facing an inordinate amount of discrimination and strife in your life! Or teachers being harder on us than our non-black classmates, as was the case with

the late Supreme Court Justice and former University of Chicago professor Antonin Scalia, who routinely gave his black students failing grades *just because*. Or the fact that black women experience "35% higher rates" of domestic violence than non-black women, according to the ACLU. Oof. This is tough stuff, but sometimes you *will* feel like a badass whenever you overcome adversity. Other times, the harshness of the world will make you cry. But #*SilverLiningsPlaybook*, things are getting better. All the black people who came before you had it way worse: slavery, lynchings, and Jheri curl juice sweat gushing down their faces like blood did out of the elevator in *The Shining*. So take advantage of the now and kick some ass!

2. **Your White Coworkers May Be More Enthusiastic about Black History Month Than You.**
How can you tell? Well, the warning sign is usually pretty clear: They will come over to your cubicle and start doing a crappy barbershop quartet rendition of "Rapper's Delight." When this happens, just remain calm. Remind them that Black History Month is not daylight saving time, so they don't need to set their

Pandora station to the Sugarhill Gang as soon as the clock strikes midnight on February 1 to show that they're down with the cause.

3. **Halle Berry Is Prettier Than You.**
That's just science.

4. **Every Once in a While, a Non-black Person Will, Apropos of Nothing, Tell You about the *One* Black Person to Whom They Would Say, "Yes to the Sex," Which Is Obviously the Spin-off to the TLC Show *Say Yes to the Dress*.**
This is only being said to you in hopes that you will be so moved to award him or her with the Purple Heart for their bravery. Yes, you will want to punch this person in the face. Don't, but I totally understand if you do.

5. **Sometimes—and by "Sometimes," I Mean "All the Time"—When You and Another Black Friend Show Up to an Event Together, People Will Think You're Related.**
You know how in the movie *27 Dresses*, Katherine Heigl's character spends the majority of her time at weddings apologizing for being single? Well, that's going to happen with you, except instead of your relationship status, you'll have to explain how all black

people aren't related. Hooray! Because that is everyone's favorite conversation right up there with "Whoever smelt it, dealt it," and my dad telling me he's taking the slow march toward death anytime I bring up his birthday. Fun times for everyone.

6. **When Standing in Any Sort of Line—at the Post Office, DMV, Grocery Store, etc.—Old Black Ladies Will Randomly Hum What You Think Sounds like a Negro Spiritual.**

You are correct; it is a Negro spiritual. Don't question it. For OBLs, this genre of "Lawd, give me the *strenf*" music is their version of Eminem's "Lose Yourself." It gets them pumped up and ready to take on the day. So let these ladies do their thing and fight the urge to join in and show off your vocals. Just toe-tap ever so slightly as though John Lithgow from *Footloose* outlawed dancing in your town, and let the OBL be the star.

7. **Regardless of Gender or Age, Strangers Will Tell You That You Look like Whoever Is the Most Famous Black Person at the Moment.**

I was once told that I look like LeBron James. By someone who can see. Specifically someone who can see my A-cup boobs chilling at the opening of my V-neck sweater the way freshly cooked gnocchi floats in a boiling pot of water.

8. **If You're in an Interracial Relationship and You Wear a Sleeping Cap/Do-Rag to Bed to Protect Your Afro, Your Significant Other Still Has to Get a Boner Even Though You Look like an Inmate on MSNBC's *Lockup: Raw*.** Don't look this up. Just trust me when I say that this will hold up in a court of law.

Well, Crambletts (and in particular, Payton), that's it! This concludes your crash course in the world of blackness. As you can see, you'll spend a lot of time explaining yourself to other people, making sure your skin is moisturized at all times, and praying that when Verdine White of Earth, Wind & Fire passes away, no one will say you resemble him. Look, I love him, but he always wears a lot of sparkling accessories like he's getting ready to sing "The Star-Spangled Banner" at the county fair and that's a choice that not even Sophie would make. In all seriousness, I understand that the truths and responsibilities I just told you about are annoying things you're going to have to contend with for the rest of your life—to varying degrees, of course, because Payton is the one who has brown skin—but just try and remember that being black is also great. We, as a people, have overcome so much and have become astronauts, CEOs, and even the president of the United States. So, Payton, you should be stoked to be a card-carrying member of blackness. Just make sure you don't try to frame it at Michaels.

Dear Future Female President: My List of Demands

Future Female President, I know handing you a list of my demands without properly introducing myself is approaching "Kanye West creating the Yeezy fashion line" levels of overconfidence. Although, now that I mention it, I don't even know if he was overconfident. Sure, it's a little cray that he apparently based Yeezy season one off the following fleeting thought: *What if my clothes only came in Beige #267, aka* Law & Order's *Ice-T's skin tone and everyone bought them? What. If.* But what do you know? His clothes have sold out nation-wide, so it seems he was just the right amount of confident. Well, you can rest assured I am not at Yeezy level right now. I'm in the presence of your greatness and my confidence is kind of shaky like that French guy who walked across the tightrope in that documentary *Man on Wire.* I mean, *hello!* You're the first female president of the United States! I would be a fool if I weren't bugging out. It's such an honor for me to be communicating with you.

Oh, right, right. Who am I? My name is Phoebe

Robinson. I'm a stand-up comedian/writer/actress, and I'm a huge fan of your work. I've been following you ~~ever since I read that Buzzfeed article listing the [insert number] times you did [insert the thing that everyone loves about you]~~ for years. I've been told some of my best qualities include excellent listening skills, a mastery of finding the best GIF to express what I'm feeling instead of actually using words, and my ability to have a stank face locked and loaded when someone acts a stone-cold foo at Steve Madden, but by far, the best thing about me is my perseverance. I'll give you an example.

Remember on *Grey's Anatomy* when Izzie stole a heart for Denny, a heart transplant patient she fell in love with, but he died anyway? It was all very sad, but then things got ri-Donkey-Kong-ulous because months later, she started having sex with his ghost. Many fans of the show were like, "The Lord is testing me with this story line. I'm out." Not I! I was like, "The Lord is testing me? Well, good thing I brought my TI-83 calc and number two pencil. Let's do this." I kept watching *Grey's* in spite of all the gintercourse, aka ghost intercourse. I'm not overwhelmingly proud about that level of commitment, but, nevertheless, I deserve some props for sticking with this crazy plot. I mean, I stuck it out past the Izzie-lighting-scented-candles-for-sex-with-what-is-essentially-recycled-air-from-her-home's-central-cooling-system scene. I overlooked her and Ghost Denny's "O" faces. And finally, when it was revealed that the gintercourse was actually her hallucinating due to a brain tumor, I didn't dive out my window because I wasted several weeks on this story line—instead, I watched two more seasons rather than do something productive, like getting my student loan payments in order. #Priorities. The point is, Future Female President, when it came to *Grey's*, I gave it my all because I'm a ride-or-die chick. And more importantly, I want to be a ride-or-die chick for *you*.

However, in order for that to happen, you have to take care of a few things for me (and all women). So, without further ado, here's my list of demands that should be super easy for you to conquer:

1. Make a law that requires all the magazine writers, bloggers, and entertainment news journalists who insist on perpetuating the thigh-gap obsession to forever be forced to own a brand-new iPhone that doesn't fit the old charger. Forever ever? Forever ever. That way, they can't give their phone some juice and will have to live with the nightmare of their phones dying midtext, resulting in that ellipses bubble appearing on their friends' phone screens before vanishing like a David Blaine magic trick. Harsh punishment? Probs, but it seems fitting for this thigh-gap obsession they created to make women feel bad about themselves.

1A. I'm not saying thigh gap, or lack thereof, should never be discussed. Half the time I'm walking, I'm contemplating turning the heat from my thighs rubbing together into a mobile BYOSI—Bring Your Own S'mores Ingredients—station where I charge people $5 to warm up their s'mores. Now that I mention it, it seems like a good idea to try to turn this into a possible business venture with any and all of the *Shark Tank* investors. I'm thinking we can call the company Still I Thigh. It would only be open during Black History Month, and while customers cook their s'mores, I'd recite the Maya Angelou poem "Still I Rise." #BlackExcellence.

1B. In all seriousness, my problem with the thigh-gap craze is that a completely unimportant physical trait has now morphed into something that women need to aspire toward, and if they are unable to "achieve" the thigh gap, they have, in some way, failed as women. This is evident in entertainment magazines and pop culture blogs where paparazzi photos of actresses are analyzed. Generally, a circle is drawn around the space (or lack of space) between her legs, and a positive "You go, girl" or a snarky "Get your life together, you garbage Dumpster of a person" is the caption. I mean, is that all it takes to deem a woman worthy or not worthy? Thankfully, the answer is no. However, if we elaborate on the answer, we will see there are other completely superficial things that women now have to be concerned with.

There's now thighbrow (the fold that resembles an eyebrow and appears where your thigh and pelvis meet when you kneel). Before that, there was *Fight Club* torso, aka Brad Pitt's extremely fit body in the aforementioned movie. This level of fitness was universally celebrated on Pitt but, naturally, deemed fifty shades of gross and un-feminine when a woman, such as the singer P!nk, was that in shape. And I'd be remiss if I didn't mention the original subject of discussion and obsession: boobs. Literally any and all boobs because it seems whatever kind of boobs a woman has is always somehow the wrong kind OR if she is that rare woman who is #Blessed with the perfect tatas, the Internet is a-counting down to the day that age and gravity catches up to this woman and her breasts sag like a pair of Lil Wayne's jeans. In other words, the avalanche of criticism toward women's bodies seems to be a national pastime, and it just so happens that thigh gap is having its moment in the sun. And it's a moment that's contributing to women hating their bodies. Women shouldn't do that! I spent my high school years hating how skinny I was— because people used to tease me by calling me names like Sticks!—which is so unfortunate because if my current stomach was as flat as it was in high school, I'd be running down the streets of NYC, topless, offering my abs as a charcuterie board for housewarming parties. Hmm, maybe that can be a business, too. Man, I really need to talk to Mark Cuban because these business ideas are just flowing out of me! Anyway, Future Female President, please make these dum-dums in the media pay for making women feel bad about their bodies and I will be forever yours.

2. Right-click and send to Trash all the women who say they're a Carrie. Even if the woman who says this is Nobel Peace Prize laureate Malala Yousafzai, one of the most important activists of our time. No one is a Carrie. I repeat, NO ONE IS A CARRIE. And why would anyone want to be? She kind of sucks (hello, her entire relationship with Aidan), she seemingly worked about three

hours a week and was surprised that she didn't have money, and after Mr. Big, her on-again, off-again beau, stated he's tired of New York so he's moving to Napa Valley, she replied, "When you're tired, you take a nap-a, you don't *move* to NAP-A." The puns, you guys. THE GODDAMN PUNS. They were endless and ridiculous as if she was constantly competing on that game show @ *midnight* and no woman I know is about that Chris Hardwick life. So let's be real. At best, us ladies are just a bunch of Mirandas with a slightly better wardrobe and at worst, we're a bunch of Magdas, aka Miranda's house-keeper, which means we're a bunch of nosy bitches who rifle through people's belong-ings and let them know they masturbate too much.

3. OK, this is probably my most important request on the list, so if you can only do one thing, I beg of you that it's this: When you get sworn into office, yell, "I'm a feminist," and then throw your fist in the air like you're Judd Nelson at the end of *The Breakfast Club*.

3A. I get that this may seem super aggres-sive and that politicians are not supposed to ruffle feathers, but this would be the ultimate gesture to let women know you have their backs. Now, FFP, if you're Hillary Clinton, you're probably like, "Can't people tell I'm a feminist because I wear Talbots pantsuits on the regs?" 1. Please don't say "regs." So not your style, and 2. No, because, your wardrobe screams "very fancy judge at a chili cook-off in Minnesota" more than it does "feminist," so we need you to actually drop the *F*-bomb into the microphone. And when you do, so many crazy old white dudes are going to freak out that it'll seem like someone just told them there are only seven tickets remaining on StubHub for a Steely Dan concert.

If you're not Hillary Clinton, but some other white lady like Elizabeth Warren (I know she has said she doesn't want to run, but I can dream), you're probably like, "I'm different than HRC. I don't wear pantsuits." We. Do. Not. Have. Time. For. These. Games, Future Female President. There's too much in this country that needs fixing to waste time debating the obvious. A sensible pantsuit is the older white-woman political uniform the way short shorts and a headband is the uniform for the least athletic kid with the most heart on a middle school kickball team.

Now, if you're not a white lady but a woman of color who ends up being President of the United States? First of all, holy cannoli! I did not see this coming. Congrats! You achieved what seemed like the impossible and I look forward to the day when HBO makes an epic miniseries about you. Secondly, and this is going to be a bummer in the summer, but I'm going to need you to chill out. You are a woman of color (and in the coolest of cool worlds, an LGBT woman of color) and that is already enough to stress some people out/make them hypercritical of every single thing you do. So you cannot be out in these streets, scaring people by pumping your fists and screaming, "I'm a feminist," the way Al Pacino yelled, "Attica!" in *Dog Day Afternoon*. You need to be hella low key about your feminism, at least during the first term. This sucks, but them's the breaks, Madam President.

3B. With that said, don't be trifling about being a feminist. It really infuriates me when high-profile people in your position self-identity as feminists just because it's trendy at the moment and then don't do any of the, you know, actual *work* of trying to make things equal for everybody. You're going to have to roll up your sleeves and get dirty in order to create a society that takes women as seriously as the men. The type that encourages us to not define ourselves by who we go to bed with at night, but by who and what we see reflected back at us in the mirror in the morning. The type that recognizes that women are not a monolith and that they have wildly different experiences informed by their race and/or sexuality. Be that beacon of light that we can look toward. Be the feminist who will help normalize the idea of Feminism for society. Be the feminist everyone needs. No presh.

3C. I'm assuming it's pretty obvious by now that you'll need a feminist posse by your side, so surround yourself with incredibly brilliant women. Women of color, women from different educational backgrounds, women of various sexual orientations. Create an army of superwomen who have medals in badassery. Use them to effect change, then go home and catch up on *The Good Wife*. I'm telling you, don't let all the Julianna Margulies/ Archie Panjabi behind-the-scenes drama dissuade you. This show is seriously so good… shoot. Hillary, if you're reading this, you're probably like, "Uh, hello! The inciting incident in the pilot episode—politico husband cheating on wife—was kind of my life." And you are correct. Sorry about that. I'm sure you can find reruns of *Northern Exposure* on the Hallmark Channel or something.

4. The following is mainly for the Future *Black* Female President, but if you're white, feel free to give it the old college try, even though you might not get why the following is super important. Can you please see to it that *Scandal*'s Olivia Pope gets a black girlfriend? Liv makes a lot of dumb mistakes, like sleeping with the very married president of the United States. And quite frankly, living life as a side piece seems to be making her depressed. She would greatly benefit from having a best black girlfriend who can share beauty products with her, bust out the rap from the *Living Single* theme song, and also keep it real enough to tell Ms. Pope not to get emotionally attached to a guy whose Tinder-profile bio ought to be "I pass my peen around like moist toilettes at a family cookout."

5. Help the world get comfortable with the word *vagina*. I mean, in 2012, Michigan

lawmaker Lisa Brown was straight up *silenced* after she said it on the House floor when discussing reproductive rights. For some reason, people act like they have ants in their pants when they hear it, which explains why there is an ever-growing list of code words for *vagina*. My go-to is *vajeen*, which I'm deathly certain was the original surname for Jean Valjean in *Les Misérables*, until Victor Hugo rightly assumed that people would fail to see the humor in that in 1862. On TV, Shonda Rhimes introduced *vajayjay* into the lexicon to make people (and Standards and Practices) more comfortable, even though the word *penis* can be freely uttered on prime-time TV shows. (Again: Viola Davis uttering the greatest nine-word sentence of all time on *How to Get Away with Murder*: "Why is your penis on a dead girl's phone?") There are many more iterations I could list here, but the point is that playful lingo is necessary because calling a vagina by its given anatomical name makes people uncomfortable.

What I'm even more concerned with are those folks (typically men) who use a litany of pejorative slang for reproductive organs to check the behavior of men *and* women. I'm sorry, but knowing all the lyrics to Kelly

Clarkson's "Since U Been Gone" or crying when something sad happens does not mean a person is a "pussy." And calling a woman a "cunt" because she is assertive or exhibits more "masculine" traits as a way to shut her down is nothing but schoolyard bullying. (Note: I'm excluding the Brits' usage of the word, which is so oft sprinkled into conversation that it seems no more edgy than Americans saying "asshole.") In both cases, *pussy* and *cunt* are ways of shaming someone into arbitrary gender norms: to let women know they shouldn't be confident and to signal to men that being sensitive is a sign of weakness. And until they unlearn these behaviors, they will be nothing more than a bunch of weak-willed pussies or scary cunts. This is crazy. Pussies, excuse me, *vaginas*, shouldn't be the symbol of "bad" behavior; the symbol should be Donald Trump and his Cheetos-dust skin tone. Furthermore, vaginas are not weak or scary. They're amazingly strong. And they're self-cleaning. Basically, women have a Whirlpool dishwasher in their pants at all times. That's some goddamned wizardry! Screw Harry Potter! Why isn't J. K. Rowling writing a book about the magic of the vajeen and calling it what I call mine: *Dolly*

Parton and the Coat of Many Colors? BTdubs, I call my vagina "Dolly Parton and the Coat of Many Colors"—sorry, you can't unknow that about me—because vajeens, much like mood rings, change color based on mood and arousal. The more you know!

5A. Once we get folks on board with the *V*-word, then we have to move on to getting people comfortable with vaginas. That's right, you have to let white dude politicians know that when it comes to women's bodies and reproductive rights, there's a new sheriff in town. That sheriff is you, by the way, and I thank you for that, because this sausage fest needed to end a long time ago. Not just because it's absurd that women are, for the most part, left out of the conversation about their own bodies, but also because most of these clowns don't actually know how the female body works. We've all read the news and watched the reports of male politician after male politician making boneheaded comments about female anatomy, and while I did revel in seeing them skewered on *The Daily Show* or *The Colbert Report* or *Last Week Tonight with John Oliver* or *Full Frontal with Samantha Bee*, once the laughs subsided, all that remained was the knowledge that uninformed people are in positions of power, and that is scary. Remember Republican representative Todd Akin? The one who actually believes that if a woman is "legitimately raped" (whatever that means), her body will just "shut that thing down" and not get pregnant? *Right, Todd.* Because a woman's body is magical and can make unwanted sperm go bye-bye if the woman wishes it away while rubbing a Sacagawea coin. Yes, I'm being flippant here, Future Female President, but I'm not too far off from some of the loony tunes things that these guys have said. So, please, be the voice of reason, be the voice of science, and be the voice for all the other women who aren't lucky enough to have a seat at the table during the discussion about their bodies.

6. Add the following sex position to the *Kama Sutra*: RRM. You know, reverse *reverse* missionary. I mean, yeah, it's just the missionary posish, which is my jam, but it sounds way cooler because I added the word *reverse* to it. Everything sounds better with *reverse* in the mix. Think about it. Reverse 360-degree dunk? Awesome. Reverse osmosis? Perfect icebreaker for meeting Bill

Nye. The movie *Memento*? Classic because so much of it is told in reverse. So help a sister out, because I'm tired of judgey mofos staring me down when I say I'm #TeamMissionary.

7. Ban drunk people from singing "Hallelujah" on karaoke night. Listen, it's an amazing song. I loved it when it was used in a montage on *The West Wing*. I loved it when *American Idol* contestants covered it. But karaoke is not the time for slow, introspective, angelic music. It's for crushing club bangers that'll make everyone twerk so hard it's as if they just learned that shaking their butts is going to replace windmills as a viable energy source for planet Earth.

8. Have the WNBA lower the hoops. Because even though layups get the job done, they're lame. Seriously, layups look the way Woody Allen talks. Wimpy as fuck. But dunking? Oh, dunking is primal and raw and passionate. It's an exclamation point, a "Yeah, I did that. What of it." Dunking is both joyful and magical, like the feeling you get when you eat a really good piece of ham hock in a bowl of collard greens that was whipped up by a portly ethnic woman in a kitchen that's a

skosh too small and a tad too humid. The point is, so much of basketball is about dunking, and more specifically, about ending up on ESPN's highlight reel because for whatever reason, everyone loves crotch-to-face interactions in sports. We're just all like, "Oooh, look how close that one basketball player's face is to that other player's nether regions! This can either be the start of fellatio OR this can end with a tender peck like the kind grandparents plant on their grandkid's knees after the kid's made a boo-boo OR the player getting dunked on might see something in the crotch like when people swear they see Jesus in a piece of diner toast and decide to change their lives." When these crotch-to-face moments don't happen in basketball, the game is basically a professional version of my brother's thirty-five-and-older YMCA league, which consists of dudes with bad backs and admirable FICO scores. That shit is boring and basically what the WNBA is right now. And the WNBA doesn't have to be. Let's help it shine bright like a diamond, or at the very least bright like the players' skin, because since it's a mostly black league, they're all wearing cocoa butter.

9. Dylan McDermott and Dermot Mulroney. Nick Nolte and Gary Busey. Gabriel Byrne and Peter Gabriel. Quit making so many white men that get confused for each other! Now, Future Female President, I'm not entirely sure how you can fix this, but something must be done because these white dudes with similar names and/or faces are too much. Older black people cannot handle this shit. And I'm tired of spending four-fifths of my Christmas vacation explaining the difference between Bill Paxton and Bill Pullman to my mom.

10. Speaking of white dudes, the sequel. Make it so that Michael Fassbender is legally required to have sex with me, which is a bill I'm pretty sure everyone in the Senate and House of Representatives would automatically get behind. I mean, don't you feel like the phrase *reaching across the aisle* was created for situations like this? And before you think he would be opposed to this, I've done the research. He's already into black chicks (his exes include Zoë Kravitz and *Sleepy Hollow*'s Nicole Beharie), so why wouldn't he be down to get with an above-average-looking black chick (read: me) who has a middling comedy

career and 750 points on her Walgreens Balance Rewards card? Also, because he's into black women, I wouldn't have to explain anything to him about black hair (but he'd still read this book because he loves me). I just get the sense that he's the type of dude who would straight up buy our half-black daughter a #BlackIsBeautiful T-shirt and help her with her book report on Thurgood Marshall. That's mad cute.

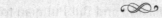

OK, Future Female President, this has been a really good talk. And yes, I'm aware that I've been doing all the "talking," but I'm a stand-up comic, so me saying all of the words without anyone else chiming in is considered "conversation." With that out of the way, let's return to you. I know you have a lot on your plate right now, but I'm fairly certain that you can handle these few requests from me. If not, I'm totally down to come to DC and help you accomplish some of the things on this list. Ooh! You can give me an office, some fancy-pants title, and I can wear fierce clothes like they did on *Gossip Girl*. Don't worry, I'll cover my own moving costs, and so you don't have to waste any brain-power, I already came up with a bunch of ideas for what my job title can be. All you have to do is choose one:

- Chairwoman of Making Sure Bell Biv DeVoe's "Poison" Is Always Played at Holiday Parties

- Secretary of... Look, It Doesn't Matter. Phoebe's Cool, So She Works Here Now. You Got a Problem with That?

- Super Dope Best Black Friend, but Not in the Offensive Way That Hollywood Does It

- Executive Director of Executive Shit That Needs Directing

Fiiiiiiiine. Ya got me! I just made these titles up on the spot right now, but whatever. We can figure out my exact title and salary later. The important thing is that I have a brand-new, primo job so I can go to my high school reunion and not have to pull a Romy and Michele by making up some crazy lie about inventing Post-its. LOL. How embarrassing, right? Like get a real job, ladies, like I did. Anyway, I'm really looking forward to working with you, and I'm even more jazzed about taking really long and unprofessional lunch breaks because working in an office kind of sucks. Not sure how you do it, but that's why you're the president and I'm just a lowly executive. Wow, I don't know about you, but I have a strong feeling that we're going to make a great team. A team in which you do all of the work, à la Nicole Scherzinger of the Pussycat Dolls, while I just look really cute, like all the other people in the Pussycat Dolls. Who else was in the Pussycat Dolls? Exactly. Am I going to ride your coattails to financial success like they did Nicole's? Of course. Will you eventually grow to resent me because I'm practically dead-weight, the way Nicole probably does the other Pussys? Naturally. Regardless, this has been, say it with me, Future Female President: A. Great. Talk. See you soon!

xoxo,

P.S. After watching the movie *Creed*, I'd like to take a moment and amend number ten above to "Michael Fassbender *or* Michael B. Jordan." Holy hell, MBJ is the heaven that's depicted in Kraft's Philadelphia Cream Cheese commercials. Yum.

P.P.S. If I'm being *completely* honest, I think I'm down for most Michaels at this point. Michael Fassbender. Michael B. Jordan. Michael Jordan without the *B* (and pre–the Hitler mustache). Also I'm a hard yes to Michael Keaton, whose real last name, fun fact, is Douglas, yet I'm a soft no to the OG Michael Douglas. Don't know why. He just doesn't melt my butter. Let's see... what other Michaels are there? Michael Ealy? Yes, obvs. Michael Bublé? Sure. Michael Strahan and Michael Phelps: Why not? And finally, I'm a "Girl, if he's good enough for David Bowie, then he's good enough for me" to Sir Michael Philip "Mick" Jagger.

How to Avoid Being the Black Friend

As someone who attended a private Catholic prep school, followed by a New York City liberal arts college, and now works in TV and film, being The Black Friend is something I'm all too familiar with. Usually the realization that I'm TBF happens around the fifth or sixth time a white buddy of mine invites me to a group hang, and I notice that my presence is like that of a singular dash of black pepper in a bowl of grits. To be fair, that is somewhat understandable; the numbers aren't in my favor. The 2013 US Census confirms that black people comprise only 14.2 percent of the American population. So knowing that, I don't expect to be surrounded by folks who look like me; however, I think it's well within reason to not be constantly *reminded* that I'm the only of my kind or (and this is far worse) be made to feel I'm someone's friend merely to fill a quota or to confirm that they're not racist. As most POCs can attest to, being used in that manner is the crummiest feeling in the world. If you're not a POC, let me explain it this way. Finding out you're a token is like when on *Maury*, the women learn that the guy they thought was the father is *not* the father, so the ladies run off set and throughout the Maury Povich studios for a place to hide, but they can't find one because every room they go into has a cameraman, so the women finally collapse onto a dusty futon near the parking garage and scream, "It's not true! It's not true!" Being The Black Friend is like that but times 1,000.

If you still need further explanation or if you're black and not sure that you've ever been TBF, let me give you some examples via my remix of Jeff Foxworthy's "You Might Be a Redneck" series. You Might Be The Black Friend If...

- You're constantly treated like a physical manifestation of the "You Might Also Like" section on Amazon.com (but only for "black people stuff," obvs): "Hey, Pheebs, I just listened to Kendrick Lamar's album on Spotify. Who else should I check out? Childish Gambino? Big Sean?" Huh? As if there's no possible way that I would suggest something other than rappers? Like Esperanza Spalding or Arcade Fire or Genesis, both the Peter Gabriel and the Phil Collins years, and want to talk about that? OK.

- Someone says to you, "I wish I was black because then I would be a really good dancer/ have a great wardrobe/tell people to kiss my black ass and it would make sense," and you'd rather hurl your body into outer space à la George Clooney in *Gravity* than listen to another second of this foolishness. #Literal-DeathIsBetterThanAWhitePersonSaying-TheyWouldGiveUpTheirPrivilegeToDance-TheSoulTrainLine

- If your white buddy treats you and the black coworker they know like two leftover socks from a load of laundry that are roughly the same size and color, but clearly weren't sold together, aka they decide you and his coworker need to date because that person is also black.

Sound familiar? Thought so. Well, my friends, this is a new dawn, a new day, a new life for me, and I'm feeling good because I've figured out how to avoid being The Black Friend, and I'm sharing my wisdom with you, so pay attention.

1. **Don't Be Black**
   HAHA. LOL. J/K! That was just a little something something to get you going. Carry on.

2. **In Times of Need Say, "Don't You *Legend of Bagger Vance* Me." It Is the Equivalent of "Satan, I Rebuke You in the Name of Jesus." Use It Wisely. Use It Often.**

Maybe your white comrade has seen too many romantic comedies in which the black best friend exists solely to be the protagonist's confidante, providing humorous takes on her pal's love and work life. Or perhaps *The Help* isn't On Demand anymore, but your white friend still needs to get his "You is kind, you is smart, you is important" fix, so he turns to you. Whatever the case may be, your name is not Frank Gehry, so it's not your job to build white folk up whenever they need an ego boost. If you're only called upon when your friend is down in the dumps or needs comic relief, then you, my friend, are like Will Smith's character in *Legend of Bagger Vance*. Nothing but a mystical and ageless 1930s caddy (read: magical Negro) who appears out of nowhere to help a down-and-out golfer find his swing again and reunite with an ex-girlfriend, and then he disappears and materializes decades later to help another white person with golf. Did this dude not know Martin Luther King Jr. was a person? Furthermore, did Bagger Vance not realize *he* himself was black? And most important, did he not realize that he was a magical, mystical black dude who has the ability to time jump? When you are a magical, mystical black dude who has the ability to time jump, you have ONE JOB: Make life better for black people in big and small ways. That's it! That's all you gotta do.

I mean, you could've skipped to the '50s and been the hype man for Rosa Parks when she refused to give up her seat on the bus. A few *Awww, shit*s would have been perfect. You could've gone to the '60s and put some Gold Bond foot powder in MLK's wingtips to help keep them smelling fresh while he's marching, and I would be like, "Great job." You could have hit up the '80s and found a black person to direct *The Color Purple* the way it should have been. No shade to Steven Spielberg; he did a good job, but he shied away from a lot of the book's ugliness in a way that a black director simply wouldn't have. The options are practically endless, Vance! Yet, you were like, "I'm going to be straight chilling in the racist-ass 1930s so I can help this white dude win a golf tournament." This is why we can't have nice things.

Anyway, the point is that if you are nothing

more than a self-help coach for a white friend, you've been Vance'd. Now, don't panic. Remain calm. Seek medical attention immediately, but if you're not near a hospital, this simple at-home remedy always does the trick:

- Say "Don't You *Legend of Bagger Vance* Me" three times and you'll be transported to your safe space. In case you were wondering what mine is, it's bottomless brunch. Literally at any restaurant. Doesn't matter. All that's important is that when I say this phrase, I open my eyes, and I'm sitting across from a Helen, two Gails, and a Denise, getting day drunk.

- Once at your desired safe space, make a George Washington Carver shrine, which is just stacks of Jif jars and lit peanut butter–scented Glade candles, and ask for serenity.

- Take a shot of tequila. Or two. Or three. Whatever it takes to make you feel like you're being covered in Anita Baker kisses.

- Repeat until symptoms go away.

3. **Do Not Start Any Friendships with White People during the Summer Months**

This may seem extreme, but hear me out. Inevitably, at some point during the summer, a white person will say to you, "Haha. I'm blacker than you," after she gets a tan and presses her arm against yours like she's doing a paint swatch comparison at Home Depot. This is not a good way to begin a friendship. You'll feel weird while your new pal will feel content in finding the one black person required to conduct this color test; therefore, no other black friends are necessary. And you know what that means: You're The Black Friend. So skip this awkwardness and wait until October to befriend some white peeps when you two can bond over pumpkin spice lattes.

4. **While Tempting, Do Not Take on the Role of Arbiter of Cool**

Don't get me wrong; at first, it'll feel awesome that people consider you judge and jury on what's dope or not. But that gets old real quick, right around the time a white friend will ask you to cosign their coolness because they know the theme song to a '90s black sitcom. Despite your pleas, they will

demonstrate by going, "Mo to the E to the—"
Stop them right there. "Mo to the E to the"
doesn't count because the *Moesha* theme song
is mostly just those six words on the repeat.
Tell that person to get back to you when they
have the 227 theme song down pat.

5. Call People Out When They Say Unintentionally and Intentionally Racist Garbage

"Hey, what are you going to do to celebrate MLK Day? Eat fried chicken and watermelon?"

No, this is not an excerpt from some
cheesy after-school special in which white
students are comically racist but it all sort
of works out in the end because the ostra-
cized black student rises above and grad-
uates with honors. Nope. This was a real
comment that was said to me while hanging
out with a few white peeps back in college.
In 2004. In Brooklyn, which is richly diverse.
And everyone laughed at it. I was told this
comment was only a "joke." Hell to the no.
I don't care how chummy we are, you don't
get to be racist in the name of comedy. There's
nothing funny about reducing me to the
damaging stereotypes that have stuck around
for centuries. Unfortunately, in that moment,

that's not what I said. Being the only person of color in the room, I was uncomfortable and felt embarrassed, so I left. Big mistake.

I should have spoken up, but I didn't, because on some level, I still cared what they thought of me, even though they clearly didn't think much about my feelings. And, unfortunately, this series of events—being wronged by another party and saying nothing about it—is all too familiar for many black people, especially black women. Often, we will not defend ourselves against micro-aggressions for fear of being labeled "the angry black woman." It's just easier to internalize these things rather than burden the offenders by calling them out. Well, I'm older and wiser, so screw that. If someone is going to be racist toward you, BURDEN them. Place upon their racist little shoulders all the reasons why their trifling comments will not be tolerated. And if they fire back that you're too sensitive or that you're angry or that you're just out to make everything about race, that's when you tell them to send all complaints and comments to my e-mail address: LookingForAFuckToGiveButCouldNotFind OneSoGirlBye@ gmail.com.

The same goes for the less offensively rude

stuff, like someone stating that you're not black because you speak in a certain way, eat certain kinds of foods, or know how to swim. While these are not likely to ruin your day, these comments fall in the column of lazy-ass ignorance, right underneath "the batteries in my remote died and I don't feel like getting up, so I guess I'm watching *Degrassi* for the next two hours." While I understand that half the time people are merely regurgitating whatever nonsense they heard from family, friends, and the media without thinking, it doesn't change the fact that they repeated it, so they cannot deny culpability. So it is up to you and me to call out this behavior every time it transpires. If the offenders are good people who made a mistake, I will allow you to find the tiniest of fucks to give about their damaged feels. And if after you present that minuscule fuck and they still don't get why they're in the wrong, or try to defend themselves, then, by all means, tell them to e-mail me at the above address and I'll educate them myself.

6. **Do Not, I Repeat, DO NOT Cosign Non-black People Singing the *N*-Word around You Because Y'all Are Listening to Rap**

Because you will now be the go-to black person when they need approval to do other ignorant, racially insensitive things. So if anyone tries to get away with rapping the *N*-word to your face, I give you permission to snatch all the hairs off their chinny chin chins as well as the rest of their body. And they can spend the rest of the evening trying to piece their hair back on themselves like they have to papier-mâché together a piñata last minute for a *quinceañera* they didn't know they were hosting.

7. **Don't Let February Turn into a Twenty-Eight-Day Press Conference in Which You Are the One Answering All the Questions**

Most black people have experienced this moment: The teacher brings up the civil rights movement and all your classmates are staring at you the way groups of married couples did with one another during 1970s key parties while deciding if they wanted to play a game of "Pass the Peen." Everyone is waiting to see what you're going to say about some of America's darkest times, and it becomes *super uncomfortable*. Your classmates and teachers aren't entirely at fault, though. Folks like Jesse Jackson and Al Sharpton, who seem to be summoned every time three old black church ladies say, "Oh, Lawd," in unison while fanning themselves, rarely miss a chance to speak for the entire black community, whether that is asked for or not (and often it isn't). So the assumption that black people are a monolith and that any one of them, including you, can speak on behalf of all blacks is slightly understandable (but still not OK). I urge you to resist the peer pressure. Don't be the spokesperson just to get everyone to stop staring at you. You'll end up frustrated, and your fellow students and teacher will erroneously believe what you said is how all blacks feel about a particular topic. Instead, do what I do when someone asks me to sum up the opinions of the nearly forty-five million black people who live in this country: Ctrl + alt + del the conversation and shut it down like it's a Dell computer.

8. **Tell People to Take Off the Kid Gloves**
Once I was getting ready for a first date, and a white girlfriend of mine said to me, completely innocently, "You can use my

makeup if you want." Sigh. I get that there are good intentions behind the whole "I don't see color" theory, but it's makeup. Makeup's whole jam and jelly is painting one's face with colors that will make it look like she woke up like dis. But if I wear white people makeup foundation, I won't look like I woke up like dis, I will look like I motorboated a mound of cocaine, Tony Montana–style.

This makeup scenario is just one example of many situations black people go through when others pretend that race and racism don't exist. Of course, this hypercorrection is born from good intentions, but it's still not helping matters. When others pretend that they've never noticed you're black, or tense up anytime the word *black* is mentioned, then they are treating you like The Black Friend, aka their "special" friend. No one likes being the special friend because the special friend is the person everyone has to tiptoe around for fear of offending him or her. It's the person who ends up being the example that people can show to the world and go, "See? I'm so enlightened because I'm friending the eff out of this black person who I didn't even notice is black, by the way." It's the person who is treated as a fragile object and not a person.

Well, guess what, kid glove wearers, black people aren't fragile. History has proven that by now. So take off the gloves, put them away, and help your friend, who happens to be black, pick out some blush from the Iman collection.

9. **Do Not Keep Talking to the Devil's Advocate Guy or Gal (aka DAG)**

I'm not against playing devil's advocate, because a lot can be gleaned from it. However, when it comes to topics such as homophobia, sexism, and racism, a particular kind of DAG tends to rear its ugly head. This person isn't interested in having a fruitful discussion that will enrich everyone involved. Nor does he have any intention to have an open and frank discussion about a difficult subject. This person is simply a shit starter, someone who is bored and wants to derail a conversation or has some inner rage that he's dying to unleash. During my days of blogging about race, I have encountered this person often. They start out as seemingly run-of-the-mill people, perhaps sharing slightly biased statistics, but asking enough questions to make it seem like they are open to exchanging ideas. Eventually, though, DAG will lose their cool and reveal themselves for who they are. I'll give you an example.

My work wife, Jessica Williams (my cohost on *2 Dope Queens,* as I mentioned previously, but you may also remember her from her work on *The Daily Show*—or as the author of this book's foreword), and I were once interviewed on HuffingtonPost.com, and we discussed how the entertainment industry is simply more difficult for women of color. This is not a refutable fact. Just look at who's being cast in TV shows and movies, and it's apparent that many roles tend to go to actors who are the color of the doves that cried in that Prince song. Within hours of this interview being published and shared on Facebook, comments were flying that I just wanted a handout for being black. One DAG in particular was insistent that blacks weren't the only ones who were oppressed or have struggled in and outside Hollywood. Jews have struggled as well, you know? The Holocaust? (Side note: I love how he clarified that he meant the Holocaust, as if I would have no idea what he was referring to.) He continued on, stating that Jews don't talk about their oppression every day; rather, they worked hard to change their fortune. He still has struggles, but they don't *define* him. Right. OK. Not to be crude, but unless Hitler was creeping over your crib à la Wilson from *Home Improvement* and giving you night- mares by singing haunting renditions of "Itsy Bitsy Spider," then the Holocaust is not *your* struggle, twenty-two-year-old Jewish dude. Pointing out how modern-day institution- alized racism prevents blacks from getting jobs and paints them as angry, scary, and a menace to society by the police until proven otherwise is not *me reveling in victimhood*. It's acknowledging the current environment as the first step in attempting to change it.

Anyway, dear reader, this gentleman and I went back and forth and as you can guess by now, I got ensnared in Devil's Advocate Guy's trap. Thankfully, there's a thing called the Block button on Facebook. And I have to say never does it feel so sweet as when you use the Block button to Heisman a Devil's Advocate Guy (or Gal) outta your business.

10. **Take a Picture and See How Everyone Responds**
This is the true test, y'all, if you want to find out if you're The Black Friend. Historically speaking, when color film in photography

was invented, technicians relied on what is known as Shirley cards, which are named after the first woman who posed for these cards. Shirley was, of course, a pale-skinned white woman. As a result, non-white people have been screwed ever since when it comes to photography lighting. Speaking from personal experience of doing talking head shows and web series, it takes about twice as long to get my lighting correct as it does for the white people on camera. Now, I'm not complaining; I'm happy people are taking the time to make sure I look great and not like a shadow that has a voice. Unfortunately, the same is not always the case in nonprofessional situations.

In regular old life, people take group photos to post on Instagram without the help of professional lighting. And I find that a photo of myself with a bunch of white peeps quickly turns into a game of "one of these things is not like the other." Essentially, the picture comes off like the beginnings of a solar eclipse. I'm all dark and shadowy and encroaching on the face of the white person next to me. This is not a good look. But this is where the test comes in. If the white people checking out the photo keep it real by saying,

"You know, let's take that over again," then you know they have your back and want everyone to look good. If, on the other hand, they look in their pocketbook and find nary a fuck to give about them looking amazing in the picture while you look like the inverse of *The Nightmare before Christmas* skeleton head, then you are The Black Friend, and not their actual friend.

Well, black reader, that's it! You know the path to leading a life free from the unbearable weight that is being The Black Friend. If anything else comes up that I didn't mention, just follow your gut. Say you're in your job's break room during lunch and a coworker jokes that since you're biracial, you don't really count as black. Feel free to say, "Excuse me, what is this shit," with so much fire that it defrosts the Lean Cuisine she's holding in her hand. Or let's say a guy expects you to be an expert twerker, simply because you're black. You have my blessing to Hadouken him, *Street Fighter*-style. Or perhaps it's Halloween and you see a group of people dressed in blackface get out of a car and go into a party. This makes you want to key their car like in that Carrie Underwood song and then brag about what you did on social media. Well, I wouldn't incriminate myself like that, but I'm not here to judge your journey, OK? Now go forth, conquer the world, and join a ragtag crew of multicultural friends that will make the Planeteers look like a group of scary, identical blond kids from *Children of the Corn*. Do it!

Uppity

~~

At the last Black People of America meeting, we reviewed the Official List of Things White People Shouldn't Do to Black Folk. Obviously, the biggies—no bigotry, slavery, racially motivated murder, racial slurs, profiling, or cultural appropriation for their own gain (ahem, Iggy Azalea)—needed no updating. But then there are more subtle things that need to be added to the list: Don't use the last of the cocoa butter, talk during an episode of *Empire*, or attend a black family cookout and say Lionel Richie blows. I mean, you're really asking to get stabbed with a Capri Sun straw if you say anything negative about Richie around black people. BTdubs, if you're wondering if there is actually a physical list, the answer is yes, there is, and, no, I'm not telling you where it is. Mainly because I don't know where it is. Only Danny Glover does. But what I *do* know is that Glover is solely responsible for amending the list. If, for some reason, he's unavailable, it's been decreed that we tuck the amendment(s) inside Aretha Franklin's hat that she wore to the 2009 President Obama inauguration and then shoot the items into the sky via a missile launcher that Glover has preprogrammed with the coordinates of where the list is located.

Anyway, at the next official BPA meeting, I'm asking that the following be added to the list: Never, in front of one thousand people, tell a black person she comes off as too smart and, therefore, less likable. No, this isn't some random suggestion. This is a very real thing that happened to me, and to this day, it gives me Vietnam-esque flashbacks because it's probably one of the most cringeworthy things I've ever experienced.

A few years ago, I was in LA for what I thought would be my "big break" in stand-up comedy. To be clear, big breaks do not exist in comedy. There's just a lot of failure offset by brief glimmers of success that keep comics going until things start changing for the better ten, eleven, twelve years into the business. But when you're almost six years in, as I had been at that point, and your checking account is dire, the idea of a "big break" seduces you. And in my case, this trip to LA was the big break that metaphorically had me splayed out on the bed while I cued up Keith Sweat B-sides and waited for it to have its way with me.

The big break was the chance to appear on a major network program, a televised stand-up competition judged by three comedians with multidecade-spanning careers. Yes, it was reality TV, but there wasn't going to be any drama, bullshit, or games, the network executives promised. Instead, the show was going to showcase unknown comics, giving them exposure that would push their careers to the next level. It quickly became clear the show was Grade A bullshit, had more games than Milton Bradley, and would rival Telemundo in the fake drama department. However, I was so enthralled by the "big break" fantasy that I disregarded all warnings from other comedians, and repeated Oprah-isms to myself: "live your best life," "own your own truth," "believe it is possible and it will be." Look, I'm not blaming Oprah for what happened to me, because sometimes you just need to repeat these mantras while wearing flowy pajama sets and lighting $15 candles. This was not one of those times, though. This was more like one of those "skip town, change your name, get a pixie cut, train with a boxer for several months, and then go back and beat the ever-loving mess out of your ex" type of situations. This show was going to be a dogfight and I was ill prepared.

The night of the stand-up showcase, I nervously waited in the greenroom, picking at the buffet-style dinner compiled from a grocery store's frozen foods department. Some of the other comics were anxious as well, while others relaxed and cracked jokes, seeming cooler than cool. Regardless of their mental state going into it, after each performance, every comic came back to the greenroom slightly disappointed. Confused. All these jokes were supposed to *kill*—the producers had approved the sets beforehand—yet the judges dismissed the comics the way a fey king would a servant. Still, I believed it would be different for me, because this was my shot. Hello! I even bought an outfit just for this occasion, which is a textbook Carrie Bradshaw move if there ever was one, as if new outfit = everything will go perfectly at the big event. Nevertheless, I was feeling good and looking good, and I was ready for what came next: the preinterview with the producers. At least, I thought I was ready.

You know those moments backstage on reality TV shows where contestants talk about how they're participating in this dance/singing/cupcake-making competition for their kids or how they can't believe they made it this far because they were drug addicts/homeless/called ugly one time while eating Lunchables in eighth grade and that they're going to win the whole shebang and spend the prize money on their deserving parents/a big vacation/a shopping spree at Williams-Sonoma? Well, a lot of those sound bites happen *right* before you're set to perform, when your brain is essentially a bowl of goo. During my interview, I'm pretty sure I said something about how it was a lifelong dream to perform in front of one of the judges (it wasn't), that the hotel I was staying at was great (no one asked me that), and that I'm doing this for Cleveland, Ohio. That's right, I was doing this show for the *entire* city of Cleveland. I acted like I was a gymnast from a war-torn Belarus who knew that if I medaled at the Summer Olympics, I was going to bring honor to my nation. Y'all, Cleveland has the Rock and Roll Hall of Fame and plenty of Red Robins; they're doing just a-OK. Anyway, I said what I said and then it was time for me to perform.

I went on stage and did my four minutes of jokes that I had been perfecting over the past few months and it went... OK. I got laughs, but they weren't as robust as they were during my initial audition. I knew I had rushed a couple of punch lines and perhaps challenged the audience with some of my race material, but with other jokes, they seemed thoroughly on board. In my estimation, I did well enough to prove that I was funny, but I wasn't going to advance to the next round. *Oh, well*, I thought, *so much for my big break*. But a little hope still glimmered when it was time for the judges' critiques because they smiled at me. Little did I know those smiles meant: Activate "break a bitch down like an improper fraction" mode*.

---

* Before I continue, I want to be clear about something. While what they did was unacceptable, part of me believes it was nothing but karmic retribution for all the times I laughed at contestants having their dreams demolished on national television. What transpired, in some way, had to have made up for every GIF I made of a Dave Matthews wannabe getting told he wasn't going to Hollywood, or the times I've rewound my DVR to mock a *Real World* housemate whose line-reading of "I'm not here to make friends" was as awkward as a five-year-old child reading *One Fish Two Fish Red Fish Blue Fish* for the first time. And it was particularly humbling because I've been proclaiming to friends for years that if I was ever on reality TV, I would crush it. Karma is the only reasonable explanation for their behavior, right? Oh, wait. Nope. It's because emotionally drop-kicking people makes for great television. Now, back to your regularly scheduled programming.

Male Judge #1 grinned. "I just want to say that you look horrible in your head shot." *Wait. Was I just reverse Paula Abdul'd?* I thought. I didn't know that was possible, but apparently it was. Sometimes, a rich person will tell you that both your talent *and* appearance is wack.

"But I will say that you look great tonight," he continued. *Well, why did you say that other shit? Besides, what does my appearance have to do with anything?! This is supposed to be about comedy!* "You look young and fresh and approachable, but in this picture… you look old. Like, you look older than my mom."

"Yeah," the Female Judge chimed in while holding up the head shot, "you look really terrible here."

If my inner rage could've been measured at that moment, it would have hit "Real Housewife high on Percocet and wearing too-tight Spanx during a reunion show episode" level. This was supposed to be my big break, but I was, as RuPaul would say, "getting read to filth," aka getting criticized to the fullest extent. I was embarrassed. I was hurt. I was pissed. Mostly at Female Judge because she's a woman and ought to know better. Let me explain: Like two great athletes who don't play on the same team but meet up on the world stage, blacks and women have always convened at the Oppressed Olympics and given each other a friendly head nod, similar to how when I'm in line at the grocery store and I notice the person in the next checkout line is also buying lemonade. I feel an instant kinship like, "This chick also loves herself enough to not drink deeply inferior Crystal Light." The point is that I assumed, perhaps naïvely, that among blacks and women, there would be a general respect for each other's histories and struggles; thus, anytime anyone came along with piping-hot foolishness, we would have each other's backs. Not this time. Female Judge betrayed girl code and doubled down on Male Judge #1's superficiality, thereby perpetuating the message that appearance is a top priority if not *the* top priority for female comics.

The hell, Female Judge?! You know better than this! It's bad enough women have to work harder and be funnier, nicer, and more likable just to get half the opportunities some of these beard-faced, flannel-wearing white dude comics get, and now you're acting as though us lady comics also have to be "traditionally hot or beautiful" to be taken seriously? Exqueeze me! I got into comedy partially because I was *not* hot. The other part was that I realized I could make people laugh with slick and snarky comments, but honestly, the not-hot factor played a huge role. I was always the girl that made all the boys laugh, and while that never got me any boyfriends, it got me male attention, which I was happyish to settle for while they all traipsed off with the better-looking, cool girls. I'm not writing this to get sympathy or have you, dear reader, go, "Oh, no, Pheebs, you're beautiful." Y'all, there was a long stretch where I was not that cute and that's OK. It made me a better, more interesting person because I developed other skills to attract people, and one of those skills is my sense of humor and personality. Thankfully, as I have gotten older, my looks, in my opinion, have caught up with my personality, but that's beside the point. Stand-up comedy is not a beauty pageant. It's about the jokes. It's about making people laugh until they can't breathe and tears well up in their eyes. It's about living by the laughs and dying by the absence of them. After all, that is how most, if not all, male comics are judged. So the fact that female comics are judged by their funny *and* their looks is really unfair. And the fact that a woman in 2014 was cosigning this sexist way of judging other women comedians made me want to graduate summa cum laude from What Da Fuq University. Unfortunately, I said none of this to her. What I did say was: "I-I mean, um, I... I don't understand. I think I look fine in the picture. I don't get it."

"What he's trying to say is you look good tonight. And he's right. You look lovely," Male Judge #2 responded in a "you ought to be grateful" tone.

Granted, I did look different between my head shot and my appearance that day. Standing before the judges, I had shoulder-length light- and dark-brown box braids. In the head shot, which was taken a couple of years prior to the competition, I was sporting a baby Afro. In the entertainment industry (and also everywhere else), people are divided about Afros. Some love this "trendy ethnic look" which is better known as "the hair that grows out my fucking head, but thanks for patronizing me by saying it's now OK because some white execs have decided barely-not-white models with 'fros can appear in T-Mobile print ads." Meanwhile, others dislike the 'fro because they think the person wearing it is fixing to start a revolution. There is no in-between. Braids like the kind I had reminded the judges of *Moesha*, the beautiful, safe, high-achieving, and respectful black teenager who never broke the rules. It wasn't that I looked old (I didn't, and if I did, that still shouldn't matter because they were *judging my comedy*) or terrible in the head shot (I didn't, and if I did, that still shouldn't matter, again, because they were *judging my comedy*), it was that I had, at one point, looked like the kind of black that they didn't want. They made their minds up about me before I ever stepped on stage. Everything else—my performance, my preshow banter on camera—was perfunctory.

"Thank you," I said to the judges for their "nonpliments" because the only thing worse than being ridiculed on TV is being labeled an angry black woman for defending yourself. Male Judge #1 finally addressed my comedy and said I had potential. And that, folks, is what they call "burying the lede." On a show *about* comedy where people are *doing* comedy in the hopes of getting their own show that *is* a comedy, spending 99.3 percent of the time discussing a contestant's looks and just 0.7 percent queefing out a halfhearted sentence of encouragement meant the lede in this case was so buried that it might as well have been the pack of zombies in the cemetery of Michael Jackson's "Thriller" music video right before they are brought back to life for the choreographed dance break.

Female Judge spoke next. "You know, you come off as the smartest person in the room. You should watch that, so you'll be more likable." I'm sorry, but *eeeeeeww*. A woman telling another woman that she's not likable because she's smart is gross. It's a big F-U to all the women who have fought and continue to fight for ladies' equality, and furthermore, it continues the cycle of discouraging women from being as well rounded as men are allowed to be. And when race is factored in, this big F-U reaches André the Giant proportions. A white woman telling a *black* woman that she's not likable because she's smart is a prime example of coded language. In this instance, smart was code for "You're showing off your intelligence in a way that I don't believe a person of color should."

The thing is, I hadn't been "showing off" my intelligence—my closing joke was about me coveting Jon Hamm's *ham*, for Christ's sakes. High concept, that ain't. The problem was that to Female Judge, I didn't sound like I majored in Grape Drank Economics with a minor in Magical Negro Linguistics, nor did I carry myself like I was lucky to have a seat at the table. I behaved as though I believed I belonged there. While that's an attribute celebrated in men, it's constantly attempted to be ground out of women, especially those of color.

Don't believe me? Look up the press's treatment of Venus and Serena Williams throughout their careers as compared to that of John McEnroe. John was a ne'er-do-well tennis star whose tantrums were passionate and rambunctious. Yes, sports journalists wrote about his bratty ways, but essentially, he was a lovable heel, and tennis fans would attend his matches in hopes of catching a glimpse of his outbursts. As a result, his fame and bank account only got bigger. However, the Williams sisters, especially in the early going, were labeled as "too confi-dent" in interviews, or accused of thinking they were better than everyone else. Well, it turned out they *were* better than everyone else, Serena especially. The issue the press had with the ladies is that they weren't like John and people of his ilk—white, privileged, playing tennis in fancy country clubs—and that despite not having a leg up in life, they still believed they were designed for greatness. Which, by the way, is what all history-making athletes do in order to propel themselves toward fulfilling that destiny. And they are celebrated for that kind of confidence. Well, the men are. The women? That kind of behavior in them is simply unbecoming!

This line of thinking is nothing new. Far worse is thought (and said) about black people way less famous and accomplished than the Williams sisters. Unfortunately, knowing all this did nothing to make me feel better about this reality show competition. It reeked of mean-spiritedness and racism (accidental or intentional, I'll never know) and signaled to me that speaking up to a white person who just told me I was coming off "too smart" and was therefore "unlikable" was not going to go well. If I were to speak back, the magic of TV editing would do everything to ensure that the judges looked great, while making me look like some sort of ego-driven villain. So I grinned and bore it.

"OK, thank you," I said as Female Judge continued with her critique. "OK, thank you," I said as Male Judge #2 echoed the sentiment that I had to tone down the smart a skosh. "OK, thank you," I said again as the host told the audience to give it up for me one more time as I walked off stage and into the greenroom. Tears welled up in my eyes, and I tried to blink them off and thought of every tell-off from movie history and pretended I was saying them to the judges. I started with an oldie but goodie from *Pretty Woman*: "Big mistake. Big! HUGE!" From *Anchorman*: "I'm gonna punch you in the ovary, that's what I'm gonna do. Straight shot, right to the baby maker." And lastly, from Steven Seagal's *Hard to Kill*: "I'm going to take you to the bank, Senator Trent. The blood bank." They can't all be gems, y'all. But above all, the one thing that I wanted to say to the judges was this: *Might as well call me "uppity" and get it over with.*

Like Gouda cheese paired with a smooth Merlot, *uppity* was a word often coupled with *nigger* back in the day. This phrase was used to put black people who possessed qualities normally associated with white men—ambition, high intellect, ego—back in their place. Over time, blacks advanced in society and bigots realized that the advantages of saying that two-word phrase (ruining someone's day) were quickly outweighed by the minuses (sitting shiva over their now-dead social calendar because no one wants to hang out with a racist), so they lopped off the N-word and just used *uppity* as a sort of shorthand.

Despite the significant advancement we've made since the mid-1800s, the word not only still persists but also seems to be too readily available on the tongues of people who ought to know better than to use the N-word's most common bedfellow. Perhaps it's nothing more than pure naïveté on my part, but I'm baffled that *uppity* is still around. After all, we are long past the days when sidewalks were turned into water slides for blacks as police hosed them down, while white guys celebrated on the streets by doing the old-man dance from Six Flags commercials. Gone, too, are the days of blacks addressing whites like an elevator attendant would on *Mad Men*: "Hello, Miss Peggy." Same with separate water fountains, being forced to sit in the back of the bus, or burning crosses on front lawns. Yet, *uppity* is still here, hanging on, dangling from a window ledge like John McClane in *Die Hard*.

Of course, people like Rush Limbaugh, Republican representative Lynn Westmoreland, and Glenn Beck have publicly feigned ignorance about the racial

connotations of the word. This would've been believable
if these men weren't well into their fifties and sixties,
fairly knowledgeable about the history of this country,
and, most important, didn't only use the word when
complaining about black people who are well spoken,
including Barack and Michelle Obama. I mean, Rush
called Michelle Obama "uppity" for stating that she's a
fan of steak with arugula. Gasp! Apparently, for Limbaugh,
arugula is too high-class of a lettuce for the First Lady of
the United States to eat! How *dare* this black woman not
settle for week-old iceberg lettuce like she's some hipster
who has three skateboards yet doesn't own a bed frame?
Despite how ridiculous the source of their rage may be,
the message these men are sending with *uppity* is this:
Quit acting above your station, *N*-word. That is why, to
me, *uppity* is the gold medalist at the Coded Language
Olympics, blowing kisses to the big JC in the sky while
its national anthem, Drake's "No New Friends," blares.
Naturally, silver goes to *articulate*, bronze to *you people*,
and in distant last is *gringo*, which is the Polish men's
track-and-field team of racial slurs.

Let's put aside the jokes and talk about coded language
for a second. In a lot of ways, coded language—which is
language that, on the surface, seems to mean one thing to
the average person but has a different, often pejorative,
meaning to the person or group of people being talked
about—has revived racism by continuing to propagate
stereotypes with seemingly innocuous verbiage. *Urban.*

Articulate. Exotic. Basically almost any word that's used in the SATs to describe people who hang at or near a veranda can be applied to non-whites as a form of gentle racism. Coded language allows the speaker to deny any sort of responsibility unless their back is against the wall, in which case they'll generally offer up a paltry "I'm sorry you feel that way" nonapology. As for those on the receiving end? Well, at best, they are left to feel like they've simply overreacted, leading them to spend minutes, hours, days replaying the events over in their mind, trying to figure out where they went wrong, even though they're certain they are right. At worst, they stifle their legitimate concerns and complaints until the bitterness eats them from the inside. Either way, it's a lose-lose.

By the age of twenty-nine, many of my black friends had been labeled as "uppity," yet I had still managed to somehow escape that rite of passage. It's certainly not for lack of trying. For years, people have been intent on letting me know that they think *I* think I'm better than them. Of course, that sentiment is never expressed outright. Oh no. It's usually shrouded in "You can't accuse me of being racist because I didn't use any racist signifiers, but we both know what I meant" language that is so shady that the Phantom from *The Phantom of the Opera* might as well be hiding in it. It seemed no one had the courage to call me "uppity" in the light of day, out in the open. That changed one fateful Saturday afternoon on the set of the first web series I was starring in.

Like with any project helmed by a first-time director, it was a chaotic set. There were hour-long delays and a slightly stressful vibe in the air, but there were plenty of snacks, so it kind of felt like a JetBlue flight, minus a Kate Hudson romantic comedy playing in the background. In short, it was a fun, hot mess. Then it became just a hot mess.

During the long second day of shooting, everyone was tired, mentally drained, and wanted to wrap for the night. White Director (this is not the best name I could come up with, but also it gets straight to the point, so let's roll with it) wanted to shoot my close-ups next. Trying to be a good actor, or at least what I thought was a good actor (which was based off the *Inside the Actors Studio* Q&A's I watched), I wanted to have my lines completely memorized, as opposed to staying "on book" during takes or having someone from the crew feed me my dialogue. So we actors tried to rehearse while White Director, who was most likely stressed about how long the shoot had been going, dissuaded us from rehearsing so we could launch right into shooting.

I could sense his tension and that he wanted to get a move on, but I knew I wasn't ready. And his anxiety was only making me doubt myself more. *I don't have my lines down. I thought I did. But maybe I don't?* I took a breath and then finally spoke. "Sorry, I know you're ready to go, but can I please have five minutes to go over my lines?" I asked.

"You don't have to be all uppity," White Director snapped.

At that moment, everything slowed down. It was as though I got shot with a tranquilizer dart, like Will Ferrell in *Old School*. My skin felt hot, and I couldn't think. Now, 98 percent of the cast and crew on set didn't hear this exchange, as they were busy adjusting lights, fixing their wardrobe, or eating, but one of the black actors in the room did. We exchanged that "Did some racist garbage just happen?" look, which is often confused for "Did Aunt Bess really bring her cold and soggy macaroni salad to the BBQ? Again?" Anyway, that look was all I needed. I knew I wasn't crazy and what just happened really did happen. I was acting for free (as was the rest of the cast) and this is how I'm going to be treated? Oh, hell no.

Regardless, I went on autopilot and powered through the scene. Once "Cut" was yelled, I walked off set and immediately vented on Facebook *before* complaining to the actors, which is how the world works now. Then I returned to set, finished out my day, and we wrapped. White Director was now being chummy with me as if nothing happened, but eventually, it dawned on him that I was not myself. He pulled me aside to a bathroom to chat. I explained to him the *uppity* situation via a short mathematical equation:

Your white skin + the word *uppity* being said to my face = me fist-punching the air like I'm getting my Billy

Blanks Tae Bo on. Or in simpler terms: You done fucked up, buddy.

Now, sometimes when people get caught with their hand in the proverbial Toll House cookie jar, they will eat every damn cookie and then vow to go to the gym later—in other words, they continue to do the hot mess behavior, but promise to get right with Christ in the morning. Other times, folks will just power through like a train whose brakes are out of service and just keep moving like nothing happened. But neither of those things happened here. White Director threw me a curve ball: He gave me an apology deep-fried in white guilt. And not the good kind of white guilt—you know, the type that gave the world Macklemore. White Director's apology was instead full of Hugh Grant stutters and bleeding heart sentiments. It. Was. Uncomfortable. And like all white guilt apologies, there were several stages.

First, this is disbelief:

Phoebe, I didn't—did I say that, really? I can't believe I'd say such a thing.

Y'all, remember on *Sex and the City* when Charlotte dated that guy who could only orgasm by saying, "You fucking bitch, you fucking whore," but he had *no* recollection of saying that and was just like, "Oh, I thought we had tasteful missionary sex and then watched *The McLaughlin Group* and went to bed?" Looks like that same confusion happened here. Apparently, White Director had a blackout à la Abbi on *Broad City*—emphasis on *black*, hee hee—except instead of wearing a fedora and singing jazz, WD was calling me uppity, then returning to his normal self to talk to me about the Knicks as if nothing trifling just went down.

Now, as I continued to explain what transpired and why it was completely inappropriate and unprofessional, WD's disbelief faded away and denial settled in:

This is awful. I couldn't have—I would never say a word like that. I know better than that. I'm from New York—

LOL.gov.

My wife and I are good people—

LOL.net.

We have kids, and we have instilled in them what's OK and what's not OK.

LOL.edu.

I don't mean to be disrespectful here, but his line of reasoning is too ridiculous to be taken seriously. First of all, people need to stop acting like racist behavior only happens within a three-block radius of Paula Deen's house. Ignorance exists everywhere, including liberal bastions like New York City. Second, saying that he and his wife are good people means *nothing*. How can I verify that? I'd never met her; I'd only seen a picture of them posing like they're about to go white water rafting, and I guess good people like that? But Jeffrey Dahmer could have been into white water rafting. I don't know his journey. The point is just because White Director married someone who looks like she models for Aerosoles doesn't mean he wouldn't say something racially insensitive. Lastly, letting me know he has a whole bunch of kids does not prove he's not racist. HELLO! Racists and bigots tend to have the *most* kids. The Duggars had *nineteen* children; meanwhile, billionaire philanthropists Bill and Melinda Gates peaced out after baby number three. This logic was not gonna work here, though it was a valiant try, I suppose.

After his failed attempt to use his family as a proof-of-purchase receipt from Not-Racist-R-Us, reality set in:

Oh my God. I can't believe it. I did say that. I'm so sorry.

HAHAHAHAHA forever.

Of course, I didn't laugh in his face, just in my mind, as he fumbled out an apology. We then bro-hugged it out, and I mostly forgot about the situation—that is, until he "John Cusack in *Say Anything*'d" me. Instead of standing on my lawn while holding a boom box playing Petey Gabes's "In Your Eyes," though, he called me repeatedly and left a guilt-drenched voice mail, rehashing the conversation we had and asking for a chance to talk to me again to prove "how much of a good guy" he is.

Just when it seemed like it couldn't get any worse, he called the black female executive producer on the web series to inquire whether calling me "uppity" was really as bad as I said it was, or if it was just a misunderstanding. I'll tell ya, only with racism, sexism, and homophobia do the perpetrators of those injustices seek verification that what they did was actually an injustice. If you think I'm being harsh, think of it this way. When White Director called the black EP, he wasn't really concerned with getting further educated about his actions; he was doing that trifling thing of looking for that *one* black person to cosign his foolishness, so he could be absolved of any wrongdoing. "See? This black lady said it's OK, so I'm good!" Yeah, no. Much like the person who promises to end their subscription to Tidal after the free trial is over but forgets and is now paying $20 a month to watch videos of Beyoncé being bored by her own hotness (What? Just me?), the lone person of [insert disenfranchised group] who is all too eager to give a thumbs-up to ignorance toward their group is not to be trusted. Run, run, far away from him or her, and say what President Bartlet once said on *The West Wing*: "Stand there in your wrongness and be wrong and get used to it." White Director did not do this. After speaking with the black EP, he had her call me to talk about the situation—a situation that, at this point, seemed to have left less of a mark on me than it did on him. And that's not because I was completely unaffected by being called "uppity." It definitely stung; however, when you are a person of color in this country, you learn early on that you cannot fall apart every time something racially charged happens to you. You just have to be resilient or you won't survive.

When we spoke, the EP took my side (duh), and I could tell that she hated being stuck in the middle of this situation. I explained to her as I had to him that I was fine and had moved on, so it was all good. She was pleased, I was O-V-E-R it, but there was still the matter of his emo voice mail. I decided to return his phone call a couple of days later. He apologized again and then the conversation segued into this:

White Director began, "I have just been so sick, feeling absolutely awful about saying the word *uppity*. I honestly had no idea of the cultural sensitivity to that word."

I replied with a simple *mmhmm*, which I suspected put him more on edge than if I let him have it, so he continued.

"I just want you to believe that I'm not rac—I would never say—I just, I'm really embarrassed. This is not who I am."

"'Kay."

A few moments pass.

"So... I sent you a friend request on Facebook, and I saw that you posted what happened on Facebook. And I know you didn't mention my name or anything, but God forbid someone saw it and was able to figure out you were talking about me, you know... and then it's like, 'Oh, God. I don't want to work with that guy.' Especially because we're trying to shop this web series around—and I know you didn't say my name—but the status is time-stamped and someone can put two and two together based on when the shoot happened... and, again I know you didn't mention my name—but can you take the status down?"

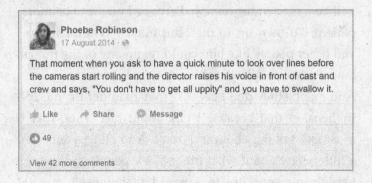

Phoebe Robinson
17 August 2014 · 🌐

That moment when you ask to have a quick minute to look over lines before the cameras start rolling and the director raises his voice in front of cast and crew and says, "You don't have to get all uppity" and you have to swallow it.

👍 Like ➤ Share 💬 Message

👍 49

View 42 more comments

Wait. What?! This is not how white guilt works! Where's my new Macklemore song? White Director's white guilt straight up rope-a-doped me into thinking that he was remorseful, when in actuality he was really concerned about his well-being. I want a refund! And I also wanted to cuss this guy out, yet for some reason, I didn't.

Maybe because my mama raised me better than that. Maybe because I was on my way to a stand-up show, and I didn't have time. Or maybe because I simply didn't have the strength to yet again explain why eradicating racist behavior is more pertinent than being called out for doing the racist action, or how even minor things like calling someone "uppity" is poisonous to their psyche, or how just because one does not lead a lynch mob or scream *nigger* doesn't mean that they don't have ugly preconceived ideas, thoughts, and opinions about different races, only to then explain all this over again after the next transgression because, of course, there will be a next transgression. Perhaps I ought to be more patient, I'll own up to that, but maybe White Director and other people like him could retain any of the things I, and other people of color, try to tell them about race. And maybe they don't because they're under the misapprehension that because I talk about race a lot, that I must *love* talking about it. I don't. And I'll let you in on a little secret about what other black people rarely say: **Explaining your life to a world that doesn't care to listen is often more draining than living in it.** And that day, on that phone, I was tired of it, so instead I chose to feel sorry for him.

I felt sorry that he cared more about someone thinking he's racist as opposed to correcting the behavior that would lead someone to feel that way. I felt sorry that after asking two black people to explain why what he did was wrong, he learned nothing from either of us. And most of all, I felt sorry because he was so self-absorbed, he will, most likely, do something like this to someone else—and that person might not be able to handle it as well as I did. And when I couldn't feel sorry anymore, I just wanted to laugh because this bizarre rite of passage of being called "uppity" wasn't even mine to claim at this point, because he had made it all about him. I was just a witness to his emotional breakdown. I was also concerned: Since there were more episodes to shoot, how would the dynamic change on set? What would happen if I left the show? How would that affect the crew? How would my character's absence be explained in the remaining episodes?

After a while, I told myself to stop with the questions. I could no longer be concerned about how standing up for myself was going to impact someone who didn't care all that much about belittling me. At the same time, though, my thoughts kept returning to the rest of the cast, which was, by far, the most diverse one I had ever worked with. Who knew when I was going to get an opportunity like that again? After all, acting with a cast that was intentionally designed to depict POCs and gays as regular people is something that doesn't happen all too often. So I weighed the options: finish what I started or tell White Director I was moving on. I chose to shoot my last episode, which not only allowed me to spend more time with the sea of brown faces in the cast, but, in a stroke of luck, also turned into a paid gig. WD felt guilty enough to compensate the entire cast for the first three episodes we had performed in, marking the first time in history that reparations happened faster than the time it takes to have an item shipped to your house via Amazon Prime. In all seriousness, it turned out that being a team player paid off, literally, which was nice, but I didn't care about the money, even though I was thrilled my making a stand benefited the rest of the cast. What I cared about was my Sidney Poitier–esque stoicism that was on full display during the showdown with the reality TV judges had morphed into something different. More powerful, direct, and better.

Don't get me wrong; remaining steadfast and not letting others see you break is one version of noble. One form of brave. And perhaps given how brutal the world is, this stoicism may even be necessary and the only reliable protection one has. This protection seems to be something that comes preinstalled in me and possibly in the souls of all black folks. It allows us, much like the adamantium that courses through Wolverine's skeleton, to be self-healing in the face of the daily micro- and macro-aggressions, to remind us to carry on, my wayward son. But it turns out for me that carrying on isn't enough. Holding my head high and rising above doesn't make me feel strong or fierce. It makes me feel stifled. Almost as if I'm choking on a tiny injustice and that one of these days, the right injustice in the right shape and size is going to lodge itself in my throat and take my voice and my very last breath. Therefore, the only reliable protection for me is to speak up. On that day with that White Director, I made the choice to never again be quiet, to never again suck it up. I challenged him. And I will do it again. If that makes me uppity, so be it. At least people know I'm no longer a vessel that they can use to act out their racist feelings. They will know that I think I'm worth fighting for. They will know that I have a fire burning inside me. They will know that I'm alive.

Casting Calls for People of Color That Were Not Written by People of Color

When I was a teenager, TV and movies were my closest friends. Sure, I had homies at Gilmour Academy—whaddup Krystle, Sheena, Brian, and Wil spelled with one *l*, but in a nonpretentious way!—and we would get into little PG adventures, like impersonating our teachers when they were within an earshot of us, taking long "bathroom breaks" from any and all science classes, and seeing the movie *Pearl Harbor* in theaters *on opening weekend* because 2001 was a world in which paying full price to watch Josh Hartnett act was a thing teenagers blindly did*. But my true besties? The people who I felt understood me the most? The guys I wanted to exist so they could date me? The women I wanted to be? They lived inside my TV screen.

As a teen, my weekends were spent alternating

---

* Side note: Teens should not be allowed to blindly do things. Teens blindly doing things is the reason why the Spice Girls ever had a career and why dELiA*s was a thriving business in the '90s, even though the company spelled its name like it was one of those annoying CAPTCHA tests StubHub makes people take before they purchase concert tickets.

between watching the shows I recorded on my VCR, like *Ally McBeal, Martin,* and *Buffy the Vampire Slayer,* and renting VHS copies of movies from the library. And since I was a paranoid, well-behaved teenager that respected authority—which is the best kind of teen to be, by the way—I lived my life vicariously through these characters. Their lives were so much more exciting than mine! They got to do the things I would never do (be a gangster, like in *The Godfather*), the things I was looking forward to doing (as with any character in any movie who was having sex), and the things I was too afraid to try, but I always wanted to do (act, like in *Singin' in the Rain*). That last one was important. Watching these movies and shows instilled something in me—some desire that said, *Hey, I could do that, right? It doesn't look that hard. I mean, I entertain all my friends.* Then, just as quickly as those thoughts appeared, another voice in my head would chime in: *But you've never taken an acting class. You've never even been in a school play. You live in the suburbs of Cleveland. How the hell are you going to get to Hollywood?*

Uh, I'd fly there. On United Airlines. A-doy, I would snap back in an "I'll show you" tone. (When you're a teen from the Midwest, and you have never flown before, you literally think *any* airline is super fancy. #NoShade, but if United Airlines were a person, it would be Mischa Barton, just real basic AF.) Then the snark part of my brain would start up again:

Girl, bye. There is no clear path for you to be an actress.

You've never tried it, so how do you know if you're any good?
And why haven't you tried? Because you're scared.

True, I'd say dejectedly. And then I'd turn on another movie and get swept away, never telling anyone—not my parents, friends, or high school guidance counselor—what I really wanted to do. I just kept this reoccurring conversation going in my head throughout my time in high school, hoping that one day, I would go to bed, wake up, and magically do something, anything, different with my life.

Now that I'm older, I suspect the main reason I kept this dream to myself is because the scariest part of working in entertainment isn't doing all the work it takes to build a career, or even failing—it's *wanting* that dream in the first place. You have to take the leap and put the work in and go all in. And being all in means there is nowhere to hide. You just have to stand there, Scott Stapp–style with "arms wide open," and accept the good and the bad that comes from trying and failing and trying and failing. You have to be *vulnerable.* I didn't like the idea of that; I was far too scared to own what I wanted. But that didn't stop that desire from roiling beneath the surface. It's why I watched *The West Wing* with the closed captioning on, so I could memorize the dialogue. It's what fueled my love of award shows. It's why I watched every single episode of *Inside the Actors Studio,* mentally taking notes and imagining what my answers would be when James Lipton asked me something from the Proust Questionnaire. (Least favorite word? Easy. When someone is called "Daddy" in a sexual manner. Whenever I hear that, my vajeen dries up like an endangered lake that Morgan Freeman is going to provide narration about in a documentary.) But because acting didn't present itself as a reasonable option at the end of high school, I decided to take a more practical route: go to college in New York City and become a screenwriter or producer. Be behind the scenes. I started applying to writing programs at various Big Apple colleges, but because I was such a slacker, most schools saw my transcripts and reacted the way I do when I'm on a first date with a guy and he uses a Groupon: "LOL. No." Pratt Institute, for whatever reason, accepted me into their creative writing program, making my plan of moving to New York a go.

Though I said I wanted to be behind the scenes, deep down, I still held on to the dream of being on stage the way Gollum holds on to the ring in *The Lord of the Rings*. That's what happened, right? I have no idea; I never saw the movies because I spent the aughts watching Vitamin C's "Graduation (Friends Forever)" music video on the repeat and wondering why all the "high schoolers" in it looked like they were twenty-seven and three payments away from paying off the lease on their Audi four-door sedans. In short, the 2000s were wonderfully ridiculous and so was my freshman year. I didn't end up performing, but I wrote a lot of short stories and garbage poetry that was angsty for no reason—I mean, how hard was life if I was lip-syncing to Vitamin C in my dorm room?—and fawned over a dude who talked about philosophy all the time (barf) and wore green army pants on the regs.

My sophomore year, though, the idea of performing became a reality. Lindsay, a fellow screenwriting major, told me about an on-campus improv group she had joined and invited me to come check it out. I, like a lot of people, was familiar with improv because of *Whose Line Is It Anyway?* And I, unlike a lot of people, was like, *It must be really cool to hang out with Drew Carey. I wish I could hang with him.* #ThingsVirginsSay. Anyway, I went to one of their shows, and it seemed like fun—everyone was goofing around on stage, making one another laugh for an hour and a half. It seemed like the opposite of Hollywood; it was low stakes. So I joined the team: "The Up Top Playerz." "With a z!" We always made sure to tell people that because when you're a bunch of middle-class people, changing an *s* to a *z* is your version of a Crip walking next to a dude you just beat up. (We were also kicking around the name "Touched by an Uncle," a play on the Della Reese religious show *Touched by an Angel*, which marked the first time in history when an insensitive molestation joke was inspired by octogenarian must-see TV.) Anyway, the Playerz was where I first found an outlet for my sense of humor, and where I found a group of friends outside of my class-mates. There was going to improv parties that consisted of one-upping and the occasional girl-on-girl smooch, attending shows at the famed Upright Citizens Brigade and getting taught the basics of the art form by Chris Gethard, performing in the Del Close Marathon, and embracing the creative outlet I had been avoiding for so many years. I was hooked, but at this point, I still wasn't open about my desire to pursue a career in performing. I felt I had to stick to the plan: be a writer and eventually, maybe, somewhere down the line, put yourself in one of your scripts.

But graduation was nearing. I had no camera equipment. I had no short film scripts that I could show someone or enter into a contest or get funded. I had written one feature-length script, a drama, but I needed a job if I was going to stay in New York, and doing improv was taking up a lot of time. So I quit improv, telling myself, *That stuff was just for fun. I need to pay bills, so I need to get a job in an office. I'm going to be an adult.* Hmm. Reading that sentence now, I wonder how many other people believe that being an adult and having fun are mutually exclusive. To be fair, I understand that mentality. I, too, chose the "safe route" and did administrative work at a few film companies after graduation, telling myself I was still close to the entertainment world. But the truth was, I was unhappy. Making copies and answering phone calls was not as exhilarating as performing on stage. And when I got promoted to a more demanding job— executive administrative assistant to the president of

Picturehouse Films—I was working fifty, fifty-five hours a week, with a terrible commute, and so I had no time to do anything. No writing. No going to UCB to even *watch* improv shows, let alone perform in them. It wasn't until Lindsay (I swear, this girl is an angel) suggested that we take a stand-up class together that the idea of performing came back into my life. I mean, what a good idea, right?! Of course I was going to be like, "Hells to the yes"?

Nope. "Stand-up is dumb," I said, and went back to emotionally eating Entenmann's crumb cake and watching *The Real Housewives of Atlanta*. Don't get me wrong; I had watched stand-up specials by Chris Rock, Ellen DeGeneres, and Dane Cook before, but it never seemed like a career to me. When I watched those comics, I had a good time, but I never felt *Ooh, I wanna do that*. I always was like, "That was great. I laughed a lot. Now, back to the real world." Stand-up was just something I would occasionally enjoy, like alcohol, or an episode of Guy Fieri's *Diners, Drive-Ins and Dives*. But then Linds hit me with some real talk.

"What do you have to lose? You hate your day job. This is going to be fun! Just like our improv days. And if you don't like stand-up, it's just another thing to add to the list of things you hate." Ouch, but she had a point. I was straight up Sad-tharine McPhee, which is what I call former *American Idol* contestant Katharine McPhee because she has an incredible voice and is stuck acting in that boo-boo CBS show *Scorpion*, where she plays a waitress with street smarts (and zero book smarts) that helps a bunch of genius yet nerdy white dudes solve crimes. Like, *really*? She can't be their intellectual equal *and* have a working-class job? Anyway, I was Sad-tharine McPhee because I had all these funny chops and I was stuck in an office job that I didn't see any way out of, so when Linds dropped the truth-bomb, I knew I had to do something. And that something was getting on the phone with my parents and asking them to pay for my Carolines comedy club stand-up class as an early birthday present.

The second I touched the microphone, I knew stand-up was what I was meant to do with my life. It felt like second nature, even though I had never told a written joke before in my life. I held the microphone with confidence and told my jokes loudly and proudly, and it felt exhilarating. Fear knew to fuck off forever, because I was about to go all in. I soon submerged myself in the world of stand-up: I went to open mics, wrote constantly, watched stand-up specials, did bringer shows (when you bring audience members like friends and family in exchange for stage time), you name it. I was having a blast, and all my friends could see how much happier I was. I was no longer just waking up and going to a corporate job and then heading straight home. I was more social, I was dating, and comedy was snowballing. It led to me freelancing for pop culture sites online, writing sketches on MTV's *Girl Code*, doing background work in friends' web series, and taking acting classes. After five and half years of working a day job, I was able to quit and pursue stand-up and acting full-time.

And best of all: I wasn't scared. Honestly, I wasn't. I was calm and confident like 2000s Prince when he showed up to award shows with his perfectly coiffed Afro, a cane, and a stank facial expression that said, "All y'all's grandmas know my corn bread and pinto beans recipe is better than theirs, so they need to stop trying and just live out the rest of their days talking about that one time they tried to smash Harry Belafonte at a civil rights rally." I was *that* confident.

Now, before you think this is some happily-ever-after BS, let me be straight here. Just because I'm confident doesn't mean I'm not constantly fighting a sea of others to land roles. As a comedian, you have to be hungry. I'm talking like one level below Augustus Gloop's greedy behind. Just gobbling up every opportunity to get seen. For examps, even though my agents send me on plenty of auditions, I also have signed up for a few mailing lists that send out e-mail blasts on the regular about other auditions. The more the merrier, right?

These e-mail blasts go out to any kind of actor who signs up for them and are generally a catch-all. They include notices for background parts like being a party-goer at a club or small parts with five speaking lines or less, or they are looking for folks with an uncommon talent like knowing how to shoot a bow and arrow or anything else that might be useful if a zombie apocalypse might go down*. Anyway, these blasts seemed to be directing me to what appeared to be pretty decent roles that could keep me afloat financially, and every once in a while, there would be roles for meatier, "every-woman" types. No longer are women just required to play the hot chick, the sassy chick, or the girlfriend without a sense of humor. Yay! But then... then I would read the *entire* description. Let me take the opportunity right now to say the following PSA to any and all casting directors reading this:

Please, please stop describing a character as an "every-woman," when in the character breakdown you go, "Someone like this... ," and then list seventy-five white ladies who collectively on their most tan day are still lighter than a batter of buttermilk pancakes. Y'all know y'all don't want me. I know y'all don't want me. The jig is up.

And if you're thinking the casting notices are any better when folks are specifically looking *for* people of color, you're wrong. Y'all. *Y'ALL*. These character

---

* If it's not clear by now, I would most certainly be the first casualty in an apocalypse scenario, and there wouldn't be any outcry like "Why did the black person have to die first?" that usually accompanies a death like this. People would be like, "Well, what did you expect? Phoebe has no survival skills, she's a picky eater, and she spent valuable time writing to A&M Records to request an Eagle-Eye Cherry Greatest Hits compilation album be made instead of learning how to do "Demi Moore in *G.I. Jane*" pull-ups. And yes, EEC's only hit song is "Save Tonight," but I could listen to that twelve times in a row, so... this greatest hits compilation is most necessary.

breakdowns got me running through the six with my casting call woes. These casting calls are demoralizing. They are cringeworthy. And most important, they are clearly written by folks who are not people of color. They are written by people who went half-mast in their pants one time over a barely-not-white person and feel as if that half chub is the only prerequisite needed for writing the most boneheaded, oblivious, ludicrous casting notices that are somehow supposed to make us POC actors feel grateful that we're being included.

To be clear, 99 percent of *all* casting notices are ludicrous, regardless of race or gender. I can't tell you how many times I've seen breakdowns for a hard-nosed woman who just happens to be an *undercover hottie*! So it's not that white actors are escaping the lunacy. They're not; they just don't encounter it to quite the degree that actors of color do, simply because most of the quality roles are written for white actors. As a result, folks like me are left trying to find a couple of non-embarrassing roles in a pile of crap. The one glimmer of hope is that the tide is changing. Viola Davis became the first woman of color to win a Best Actress award at the Primetime Emmys; Golden Globe winner Gina Rodriguez's *Jane the Virgin* is one of the most popular shows on TV right now; *Fresh Off the Boat*, the first show about an Asian-American family to air on network television in twenty years, is a critical and ratings success. But for the handful of wins like these, there are thousands of losing moments, and they start with these casting call notices. So, I want to give you, dear reader, a sample of what I, and many others, go through as performers when we look for roles. To protect the insensitive, the following notices are made up, but are inspired by what my friends and I have seen IRL.

Reneighaaay (Series Regular):

Sassy yet smart career administrative assistant to Ted, her boss, whose life is a mess—his wife left him and his personality is horrible—BUT he has a rotating cast of twenty-something women that sleep with him because he's handsome. Despite Ted's ne'er-do-well ways and the fact Reneighaaay is severely underpaid, she is fiercely loyal to him because she knows the loving of a good woman will change him. In the meantime, she will be by his side giving him a healthy dose of real talk. This character has no dreams, hopes, or desires of her own. Actress must be comfortable with saying "Mm-hmm" and "Uh-huh" when the writers don't have time to write actual dialogue for her.

My favorite part about these kinds of notices is that even though the character's name is pronounced *Renee*, it's spelled the way a guy says "Renee" when he's orgasming because racism makes the writer of this description bust a nut. More important, this absurd spelling lets everyone know this character is black. I supposed that's because if it isn't "clear" that the character is supposed to be black, the role would just end up going to one of the women from *Gossip Girl*.

Now that we're warmed up, let's check out another kind of notice. It's also for an assistant type of character, although this one doesn't have a name. But no worries, because the casting director *swears* the nameless character is pertinent to the plot and that there will be several scenes of meaty monologues for the actress to show off the skills she learned from taking Kevin Spacey's online *MasterClass* course:

Legal Assistant—Untitled
Jason Bateman Project

Character Description: Don't let the lack of having a government name fool you! Legal Assistant is very important to this film. She will be in the room when her boss William Henry Richardson III does some really shady deals. There's even a time when she witnesses him doing something very, very bad without him noticing that she's in the room because this is a thriller! The pressure gets to her, which explains why she copes with the stress by being rather sexually promiscuous. Note: This role requires frontal and topless nudity.

Hooray! This super-misogynistic role is open to *all* races. Clearly, this will go to Eva Mendes, but it's nice to be asked to audition for this because that means someone involved with this production wants to have sex with you. Fuckability is key to your life as an actor. Never forget that!

OK, so even though these roles are not the most desirable, at least they are presented in a pleasant and somewhat professional way. That's not always the case. For instance, when you don't have an agent and you're just starting out in the business, you don't have access to casting notices for TV series or big studio movies. So you have to look for work elsewhere. And by "elsewhere," I mean Lucifer's taint, aka Craigslist. Look, I love me some Craigslist. You can indulge in the rom-com fantasy of missed connections, you can waste time having discussions in one of its many chat forums, and it's great for when I need an "earthy" coffee table, which in CL-speak means, "A trifling heaux used to put his feet on this table all the time, so it has a slight funk smell that gives it character." But hunting on Craigslist for roles that will pump up the ole acting résumé? Good luck because most of the casting notices are just hot garbage like the following:

Interested in a role in which you are only a few years older than the lead actor playing opposite you, yet you are cast as his *mother*? Sure, you're not even thirty, but let's face it: Your insides are probably like a rotting bag of baby carrots, right? Right. So you're a mom. Thankfully, you're still attractive in the face. Role consists of standing off to the side and watching the action go down, telling your son he is destined for greatness, and that one scene where you have to be attracted to the much older actor playing your husband even though your spirit is like, *Nah, boo. I ain't feelin' dis*. You will get felt. Like literally. You will be naked during love scene while much older actor gets to grab your boobs. He, of course, will be fully clothed like he's about to go catch fish with Bear Grylls in Alaska. Ethnically ambiguous.

This is why Craigslist's "anything goes" vibe is kind of boo-boo. Lots of times what you get is less of a character breakdown and more of a dude in his Fruit of the Looms writing out some wackadoo pseudo-oedipal nonsense from his mom's basement. I mean, we all remember the disastrous movie *Alexander* in 2004 where Angelina Jolie, who at the time was twenty-eight years old... and was cast as Colin Farrell's mother even though he was only *one year* younger than her at the time. And who was cast as the dad? Old-ass Val Kilmer, who was forty-four at the time. Look, I love me some Val Kilmer. Anytime I watch *Batman Forever*, there's light precipitation going on in my vaginal walls—#HaveAPonchoHandy—but he was damn near fifty before he got cast as a dad in a movie (so it was at least in the realm of possibility that his character could have been a teen dad). But Angie Jo was still at the age when crow's-feet would come knocking at her door and she'd treat them like Jehovah's Witnesses and go, "Boy, bye," slam the door shut, and continue being young-looking AF. While this is the sort of nonsense the entertainment industry perpetuates on the regs, at least the writer of these kinds of ads gets to the point. Who needs to be insulted in a roundabout way?

Casting for commercials gets even more succinct because the world of commercials is like a factory. There are hundreds of TV shows, meaning there are tons of thirty-second ad breaks that need to be filled. If A-list movie work is filet mignon, then commercial work is an unopened and beat-up bag of Lays, in which all the chips are broken... you know, like your dreams will be because you're stuck in the hell that is commercial work. On the plus side, because commercial casting is quick and dirty, the castings don't waste your time, and present you with just the facts, Jack:

Role Name: African-American Principal
Attire: Professional
Role Details: Nice-looking, personable, but not too dark

OMG! You guys, you don't actually think this is racist, do you? It totally isn't. It's just one silly misunderstanding, as a rep for Acura explained when the casting director posted a notice very similar to the above. The rep claimed that the "not too dark" request was simply made because being dark would make lighting and special effects more difficult. Nope.edu. If the BBC can light Idris Elba for Luther so he looks like a delectable blueberry tart from Giada De Laurentiis's kitchen, then y'all can light a garbage ad that's going to air during Jane the Virgin commercial breaks.

But let's not Panic! at the Disco (can you please give it up for that amazing reference?) because not everything is Dire Straits (see what I did there?) for actors of color. Viola Davis and Gina Rodriguez are leads in TV shows when twenty years ago they would've been a basic B, heating up a Lean Cuisine, and making a "this lady needs to get her life together" face while the white female lead character has all the fun. Ditto for dudes of color. *Blackish*'s Anthony Anderson is a loving dad who also gets to discuss issues like police brutality and the N-word in funny and touching ways, and *Master of None*'s Aziz Ansari captures the millennial experience realistically because it's being written by millennials and not out-of-touch fifty-year-old white dudes. Because of this, Hollywood is more willing to show men of color as more than just thugs and goofy Others. Too bad this casting notice is still a fail because even though this MOC has a non-degrading job, the role continues to perpetuate the notion that certain men of color are not desirable:

Dr. Ryan (Recurring Character): Age range: 30s–40s. Last name, personality traits, and character motivation do not matter. Handsome, but not too handsome because he's either Indian or Asian, c'mon! Ain't nobody attracted to those kind of men.

LOL. India is a part of Asia, but who has time for geography? OK, OK, I'll stop busting balls. We should all be thankful that an Indian or Asian guy is getting a chance to work. Who cares if he's playing yet *another* asexual man?

Speaking of men, society is finally recognizing the ever-evolving world of gender identity. And thanks to trans activists like Janet Mock and shows like *Transparent*, Hollywood is being forced to expand their idea of diversity. Trans people need their stories to be shared, but unfortunately, Hollywood hasn't entirely caught up to how to make that possible, so they tend to rely on a bad habit: If you have to try, it's just easier to go with a white guy…

Jeslene (Lead): Late 20s/Early 30s trans character of color who—you know what? Never mind. We're going in a different direction. We're just going to cast Eddie Redmayne to play her.

Ah, so close, yet so far. Maybe next time! Until then, Laverne Cox is going to be the sole star who is representative of trans people of color. Nothing against Laverne—we all love her—but trans people don't all have the same life story. UGH! There should be more than one trans narrative, Hollywood! Respect and reflect the wealth of trans stories, please, and in order to do that, you need to hire more than a handful of trans actors! After all, more than one trans actor can and should be a superstar!

Let's turn it back to people like me: hilarious ladies. Every few years, there are all these articles called "Who Says Women Aren't Funny?" Or "Funny Women Are Finally Breaking into the Boys' Club." And my personal fav: "WHUT? Women Are Like Funny and Stuff? That Idea Is So Wacky That My Dick Almost Flew Off in Disbelief." As annoying as it is for the media to constantly be shocked that women can have senses of humor and be amusing to men, the plus side is that all this discussion is leading to more comical characters for women. Like this one!

Li-Nee (Horny Foreigner)

Description: Who says women can't be funny? Not us! We're taking the Long Duk Dong character from *Sixteen Candles* and modernizing it. Meaning Li-Nee is portrayed by a woman instead of a man! Neat and kind of edgy, right? Anyway, this lady's really funny, a girl-next-door

> tomboy who will look jaw-droppingly beau-
> tiful after her makeover scene. Can be gross
> and vulgar like Seth Rogen, but still beautiful.
> Should be comfortable doing some improv and
> a couple of scenes of nudity. MUST be capable
> of speaking in broken English. Only people in
> 20s will be seen.

How cool of it that whoever wrote this movie with all male characters and then at the last minute changed one of their names to something female-sounding and voilà, this means the filmmaker cares about and acknowledges women! Not! I mean, yes, we have ourselves a lady in Li-Nee, except nothing that is unique or pertinent to her female experience will be explored. And ladies and gentlemen, that's what happens when no women are involved in the writing process. You end up with a dude's idea of a woman, which is just a human being without a dong, aka John Bobbitt, for that half day it took the po-po to find his peen after his then-wife Lorena chopped it off. I mean, it's almost as though the writer of this movie hasn't met and/or doesn't like women? Oh, wait, she's low-key hot, and lucky for her, guys realize this once she makes an effort to fit within heteronormative standards of female beauty. And by seeing how men respond to her physically, she learns to love herself. No, we were right the first time. The writer of the movie doesn't like women.

Every once in a while, when you're on Backstage. com, a director will list multiple breakdowns for various roles in his movie. What's nice about this is it allows actors to see what the director's vision is for the entire project:

Beautiful Actress, Breathtaking Smile
Requirements for Lead Actress:

Highly attractive, Age 19-34

Very fit & in shape (Kim Kardashian–esque A-plus, Serena Williams-ish? Not so much)

XS size ideal, S is OK, I guess, but like...

Females, any ethnicity, but if African-American, no extensions, dreadlocks, weaves, or dyed hair. MUST BE NATURAL HAIR.

Acting Experience: Previous unpaid and paid speaking roles. An episode arc or two on a few popular television series as well as a lead role in an indie film is ideal.

Old Male Actor Needed
Requirements:

Males, Some experience (played the dancing old guy in the Six Flags commercial).

Age range: Phil Spector to Al Pacino playing Phil Spector in that HBO movie, aka old AF.

Ah, right. How could I forget? Not only do women have to be as physically fit as an athlete whose sport of choice is eating salads and having sex, but they also have to have the IMDb résumé of an experienced actor while still, and somewhat impossibly, being as young as the dancing baby from *Ally McBeal*. #Callback.

Finally, thanks to the whole #OscarsSoWhite controversy, it seems that casting directors are making sure actors of color are getting the opportunity to have Academy Award-winner-caliber roles:

Naked Slave

You will be naked. You will have no lines. You will play dead.

Motherfucker, this isn't the boat scene from *Amistad*. I am all slave-movie'd out. Hard pass.

So, this is what life is like for people of color who pursue a career in acting. We are bombarded with notices that take figurative Metamucil-infused dumps all over our hopes and dreams of having an IMDb résumé like Jennifer Lawrence's or Christian Bale's. But don't get too bummed out, because it really does get less awful the more us POCs advance in the industry and become the stars and creators of TV shows and films. I'm a prime example of that momentum. Just three years ago, no one knew who the hell I was. Now I have the occasional person reaching out to my manager/agents about getting me to audition for stuff. Granted, a fair amount of the roles are my being surprised that chicken can be fried and readily available to be purchased, but it's something. In all seriousness, I'm getting small roles here and there on Comedy Central, Amazon, and Netflix shows, and it's giving me hope that I can break through by being myself. As naïve as this sounds, I simply won't allow myself to be stuck in stereotype hell for the rest of my career. I *can't* allow it, especially after people like Shonda Rhimes have shown me that there's another way. I don't have to keep auditioning for roles that insult my intelligence or treat me as though I should be lucky to be part of the game. I can say no to an insulting casting notice because there is more out there than being cast as the sidekick to a white character, where one of my lines would be about how my friend is pretty and exciting and I'm not. Television is proving time and time again that there are more complex and interesting roles. And that is giving me hope that one day I can join my besties like *The West Wing*'s C. J. Cregg, *A Different World*'s Whitley Gilbert, *Seinfeld*'s Elaine Benes, and countless others. And when I do, I want to have something to talk about. Stories that match and surpass theirs. Looks like I might just have to create that something to talk about.

The Angry Black Woman Myth

Friends, I'm going to blow your mind a little bit: This essay, which appears here on page 212, is actually the last chapter that I wrote for this book. I know! I just ruined the fantasy that books are always written linearly. Sorry! But this whole angry black woman thing is draining to talk about, which is why I've put it off to the very last minute. I guess you can add this revelation to the list of other misconceptions about writing, which include the following:

- Authors only write when they are inspired. Sure, many written works start under the influence of a muse, but let's get real: Books get completed because hard work taps muse on the shoulder like a WWE wrestler does his tag-team partner during a match and takes over to do all the dirty work. Please note: Wearing shiny spandex wrestling trunks while writing is not required, but go for it. I'm not here to judge your journey.

- All writers are tortured. Case in point: A friend told me about New Year's Eve yoga, which is a regular yoga class that culminates in a kombucha toast, and I actually said, without any sense of irony, "That sounds amazing. I should do that." I'm not a tortured soul; I'm a white neighborhood gentrifier trapped in a black person's body, and my neighbors of color have no idea. The phrase *The call is coming from inside the house*? It's about assholes like me.

- Writers are seductive, great in bed, impeccably dressed, and live in loft apartments that are expertly decorated. This stereotype exists because pop culture has tricked us into believing this nonsense. Take, for example, the rom-com *Alex & Emma*. In it, Luke Wilson plays a struggling novelist who allegedly has no money, yet he has a bomb-ass crib and he's always dressed like he's on his way to pose with a goddamn golden retriever for an L.L.Bean photo shoot. No. Just no. People who look like the wickedly handsome Luke Wilson do. Not. Write. Books. Luke Wilson is too busy being all Luke Wilson–y with a "totes casual" hotness that makes ladies do the "happy baby" yoga pose in his presence. #YogaCallback. So, no. Writers are not like Luke Wilson. Writers are like me: clothed in pajamas and writing while covered in blankets/hunched over a desk with sleep breath and Cheez-Its crumbs that have somehow worked their way *inside* the crotch of their underpants.

So the writer life is not cool or glamorous, OK? Now that's out of the way, what else can we talk about? Oh, right. It's in the title of this essay. The angry black woman. That's why we're here. Heh. I know. I know. I'm stalling. And I'm stalling because I've been on this planet for thirty-one years, and I don't *really* know how to discuss the topic without feeling conflicted. If someone were to ask me, "Are you an angry black woman?" I would reflexively respond, "No. I'm not," without flinching or taking any time to truly think about what is being asked, and that's troubling. After all, if I can spend forty-five minutes deciding what tapas restaurant to go to, then shouldn't something like whether or not I'm an Angry Black Woman—and all the baggage that comes along with that phrase—be carefully considered?

Angry. Black. Woman. Just three little words, but combined, they become a scarlet letter, tarnishing its wearer as hateful, irrational, emotional—someone to avoid at all costs. This trope, which seems to haunt every black woman on the planet, was popularized back in the 1930s thanks to a character on the radio show (and subsequent TV show) *Amos 'n' Andy*. Sapphire, the emasculating, domineering, and nagging wife of George "Kingfish" Stevens, gave birth to the notion that black women were ungrateful and hard to please and created a mold for which lazy TV writers could cook up other stereotype-laden characters, from Aunt Esther on *Sanford and Son* to reality TV shows like *Basketball Wives*. Despite its preeminence in pop culture, scholars Dionne Bennett and Marcyliena Morgan suggested in their 2006 paper "Getting Off of Black Women's Backs" that social and cultural researchers who spend careers studying trends don't even bother to investigate the idea of the angry black woman:

> The stereotype of the angry, mean Black woman goes unnamed not because it is insignificant, but because it is considered an essential characteristic of Black femininity *regardless* of the other stereotypical roles the Black woman may be accused of occupying. These stereotypes are more than representations, they are representations that shape realities.

I don't have official empirical data to back up this claim, but based on my life experiences, it's hard to refute what Bennett and Morgan wrote. The concept of the Angry Black Woman has affected how people view me. Take this instance. A few years ago, a white male comic introduced me by saying, "Do you guys like pussy? Well, this next person has one." After my set, I walked off stage and politely told him what he did was inappropriate and unacceptable. He responded loudly so everyone in the audience could hear: "WHOA! Calm down. Don't need to get all *angry black woman* on me. But that wouldn't be the first time that happened to me." Huh? I mean, I approached him with "white lady dealing with unsatisfactory customer service" speak, which is just one notch above "baby giggles while farting" on the Innocence Richter Scale. Still, all he saw was a feisty black woman who was flying off the handle and causing a scene. Yet while his outrage at how *I* rejected his objectification of my body was upsetting—guess what?!—I couldn't actually get angry because if I did, then everyone in the room would think, *See, she is an angry black woman. He said it and she just proved it.*

UGH! This sort of thing happens all. the. time. Something completely disrespectful will be done or said, and black women have two options as a means of response: 1. Suck it up, or 2. Hulk-smash everything because the mistreatment is *only* happening because the person(s) refuses to see black women as humans—and more than anything, we just want to be seen. But if we Hulk-smash, then we're forever known as the angry black woman, who is to be avoided at all costs or placated with a "there, there" tone that's used on *Dog Whisperer with Cesar Millan*. Who wants option two? So, the answer to the question "Are you an angry black woman?" is *no*, I am not. And no, that was not an angry denial of my being angry. See? *This is why I have been stalling*. Because this question and this label unfairly positions a black woman at a disadvantage, where she becomes either flustered or unintentionally defensive.

Now that I think about it, the relief I feel when I deny the label is a little suspect. It seems to come less from a place of truth of evaluating whether I'm angry and more about my need to avoid that evil stereotype that some people assume I am. Oof. That was rough to admit. Let's investigate this a little more. If I am not an angry black woman: Why not? Society doesn't exactly make life terribly easy for black women—and yes, life is hard for everyone—but black women have their own unique battles, a Molotov cocktail of racism and sexism. We have to combat the stereotypes of being at once hyper-emotional and stoic, we have a shorter life expectancy than white men and women, we're paid less than men and white women, we're three times more likely to be incarcerated* than white women, have a higher poverty rate than other women** and, perhaps, most important, getting our hair done takes as long as the run time of the BBC's six-episode miniseries *Pride and Prejudice*. So

---

* According to an ACLU study, "black women represent 30 percent of all incarcerated women in the United States, although they represent 13 percent of the female population generally."
** AmericanProgress.org reports that the poverty rate for black women is 28.6 percent while it is only 10.8 percent for non-Hispanic white women.

how do I, or any black woman for that matter, come up against these types of obstacles and remain in mint condition? Not even be the slightest bit perturbed? That doesn't seem possible. I mean, no matter how idyllic one's life is as a POC, there always appears to be some BS right around the corner. I'll use myself as an example.

My parents have been happily married for thirty-five years. I attended a phenomenal private high school and a well-respected liberal arts college. I live in New York City. I've been in love. I have a thriving comedy career. When I order things from Amazon Prime, they always end up getting delivered a day early. When I pause Netflix for a really long time, it asks me if I am still watching, and I think it's just swell that Nettie checks in on me. Clearly, life is pretty banging right now. Yet despite all these kick-ass things, I still:

- Lose out on jobs because of the color of my skin

- Have men condescend to me in the workplace because I'm a woman

- Experience sexual harassment from both strangers and colleagues

- Have guys call me a See You Next Tuesday on my Facebook page

- Receive private messages from dudes attempting to shame me for expressing any frustration I have with how I am treated as a black woman

- Receive messages from others implying that because I have self-love I most definitely am a racist and hate all white people

- And the list goes on and on

Oof! Just writing out these few things made me a little 'turbed. So perhaps I'm a black person who happens to be a woman and who happens to be a skosh angry or a skosh angry person who happens to be black and female. That's maybe like saying, "I am flour who happens to be mixed with baking powder, salt, butter, and buttermilk and all that happens to be—"

"A biscuit," someone might interrupt. "You're a biscuit." "*No*, I am flour who happens to be mixed with baking powder, salt, butter, and buttermilk and all that happens to be—"

"Girl, you are bis. Cuit. You are such a biscuit, with a two-piece and some green beans flanking your sides while that black lady from the Popeyes commercials stands behind you, talking about Louisiana cuisine."

What I'm getting at here is that to a lot of folks, it doesn't matter that I'm multi-layered like an Au Bon

Pain parfait and have unique qualities, because as a black woman, I'm not allowed to embody various personality traits without an ugly label being slapped on me. This is completely unfair, world, and news flash: There is a distinction between the "angry black woman" label that society has used to silence and shame black women, and being a black person who happens to be woman and who happens to be a skosh angry, which, by the way, is *usually* what we refer to as multidimensional... unless that's reserved for white dudes in prestige TV. LOL. Like all black women, I am a complex person who feels the full range of emotions—happy, sad, confused, nervous, mad, curious, aroused, helpless, and so on and so on—therefore, the latter classification of black and female and angry seems more in line with who I am. Either way, the result is the same: I find myself double- and triple-checking my behavior. The idea behind the old adage of "measure twice, cut once" applies to black women except the wording gets changed to "overanalyze what you are thinking by weighing the pros and cons of saying your truth to someone who might not want to hear it, assess your surroundings (are lots of people watching you, and more important, are white people watching you?), and speak once, in a very nonthreatening manner, of course." Rolls off the tongue, doesn't it? Truly, though, there is a Predator-like mental scan that black women have to do before speaking, and even after we've done the risk assessment, things can still go astray.

I learned this lesson a decade ago and haven't forgotten it since. Let me explain.

You know how when an aunt of yours is getting ready to spill the tea to your mom about their mutual friend Deborah by saying, "Look. Deborah? I mean, she is a sweetheart. So nice. Her parents? Wonderful people. But last week, Deborah was acting like a little shit"? Well, I'm going to do that here. Pratt Institute? I mean, a very good liberal arts college that I attended. The writing program? Wonderful program. But once during my senior year, things got pretty shitty. One time, during my thesis class, a classmate wrote a play in which a black female slave said "hard pass" to escaping slavery via the Underground Railroad because—get this—*she fell in love with her slave owner's daughter.*

Let's go back to 2006, a time of *Big Momma's House 2*, the International Astronomical Union downgrading Pluto from planet status—#WayHarshTai—and me being too into the Pussycat Dolls. This was apparently also the time where this lesbian slave tale just needed to be told. After three years of reading critical theory and writing short stories and bad angsty poetry that would even make the band Dashboard Confessional go, "I'mma need you to chill," my classmates and I entered our senior year and finally, *finally*, we could apply all the skills we acquired to write a collection of short stories or creative non-fiction, a screenplay (that's what I did!), a play, or a big, fat, stinkin' pile of poems. Whatever tome

221

we submitted, it was supposed to best represent who we were as artists. Kind of like how on every season of *American Idol* there was a week where the contestants had to choose *the* song that represented them and inevitably someone would pick Smash Mouth's "All Star," which made viewers go, "Is this real life?" That's what my senior class did; we all wrote a bunch of "All Star"s because we were twenty and twenty-one and had no idea who the heck we were, so our great works were not so great. But there's a difference between a young goober and finding your voice and writing a *slavery love story* that you expect everyone to cosign, no matter how ludicrous it is.

To set the stage: The woman who wrote this slave play is white, and to protect her identity, let's call her Rebecca. A big part of this class was workshopping our material so we could get in the habit of being accountable for what we write. Meaning, a lot of beginning writers have a tendency to write a piece and then defend it by saying, "Oh, well, what I meant here was this." "What I was trying to say was that," giving people a "director's commentary" of what their work was supposed to be, rather than letting the work stand for itself. To avoid this, our work would be read aloud by someone else (or in the case of plays and screenplays, parts would be assigned to everyone except the person who wrote the work), and then we'd receive feedback from our classmates. The creator of the piece, though, was not allowed to say anything during the critique; we just had to take it in. Humble thyself, I think was the lesson here. So on this fateful day, Rebecca passed out her work in progress and explained that it was a lesbian love affair set during the slavery era, which was meant to serve as a commentary on race and sexuality today. O... K. Guys, this sort of thing tends to happen at liberal arts colleges. Kinda like when a woman on *What Not to Wear* goes clothes shopping after her first talk with the stylists and is like, "Oh! They want me to be more trendy, so I'm going to get high-waisted velvet skinny jeans, sneaker wedges, a combination of seventy-two rings, a silk top with cutouts that is layered over a gray cashmere sweater, and a yarmulke on top of a fedora." LOL. WUT. You are doing the most when doing 75 percent less would be 200 percent much more appreciated. And at liberal arts schools, people want to be so bold and so complex that they want to tackle every single hot-button issue at once instead of just tackling one thing really well. This was clearly what Rebecca was doing.

Now, Rebecca had just recently discovered that she was a lesbian, which is amazing—live your truth, girl!— and I'm guessing she *also* discovered that, like, slavery is a real bummer, and probably would've been better if slaves worked a little less and could just Greg Louganis into some muff. Honestly, with the way her play was written, if it got adapted to the big screen, it would be nothing more than a zany rom-com with Katherine Heigl as the slave owner's daughter and Kerry Washington as the "all work and no play" slave who could loosen up if she just had a little bit of love in her life. P!nk's "Raise Your Glass" would play in the background and the music would cut out just as Kerry Washington's character falls while trying to lift a heavy stack of cotton. #BecauseWomenAreKlutzes #BecauseHollywood. I'm exaggerating for effect, of course, but Rebecca's play was embarrassingly tone-deaf. As I was reading the part of the slave aloud (YEP. FUN.), it became clear that I wasn't the only person in class that picked up on that. The sound of people shifting in their chairs was audible as the play was being read, particularly when Slave Owner Daughter and Slave had a meet-cute. A MOTHERFUCKIN' MEET-CUTE. *DURING SLAVERY*?! #BecauseWhyNot.

As you probably noticed, my lovely readers, meet-cutes generally happen between two people who, I don't know, both have their rights?? If both parties have their rights, you can meet-cute until the cows come home. But when one party legit does not know how to read and is whipped more regularly than Land O'Lakes butter, YOU. ARE. NOT. MEETING. CUTE. That woman is only meeting your ass because your daddy BOUGHT her.

My senior thesis class was small, about fifteen people. All of them are white except me, which is literally the story of my life. Clearly, CLEARLY, everyone realized this play is absurd, and as I'm reading, I caught some of my classmates and my teacher sneaking looks at me, as if they want to know whether I was going to blow my lid. I did not, because, again, the whole angry black woman thing. So I kept reading and a bunch of other stupid-ass things happened, which I forget because after class, I went to the same doctor Jim Carrey did in *Eternal Sunshine of the Spotless Mind* and promptly had most of this fuckery extracted from my brain. The job was not done thoroughly, though, so as a result I have also forgotten how to ask where the library is in Spanish and anything above middle school– grade math, but that is the price one must pay when wanting to erase the memory of being subjected to the idea that a few nights of scissoring is all that is required to right that whole slavery thing. But the details about the middle of the play don't even *matter* because, here, it's all about the ending.

Slave and Slave Owner Daughter are fully in love, but Slave finally gets the chance to escape. She tells bae what her plan is and Slave Owner Daughter is like, "Nooooooooo, we're in love, though!" Slave is like, "But Massa is gonna rgre;grehtwirlht. We can't ppwutpwuew, Wingdings, Wingdings, Wingdings," because the Slave is also super dumb and can't speak eloquently. "True," Slave Owner Daughter says. The slave, seeing her precious white bae crying precious white tears goes, "rghre;gjpoj wr;f[owef m," aka she's going to tell the other slaves to go without her because she's going to stay a slave so she can be near her boo because love conquers all. Wingdings, Wingdings, Wingdings, guys. What in Harriet Tubman satin-bonnet hell is this foolishness? I'm sure you get why the ending of this play is utterly ignorant, but let's break it down, shall we?

1. Slaves did not just go around giving their owner's kin TMZ exclusives about plans to escape from the never-ending hell that was slavery.

2. If you are a white person, do not write some garbage story and heavily pepper it with words like *massa* and think that I am, as the only black person in the room, going to happily read that mess aloud like I'm gunning for Meryl Streep's spot as the Queen Bee of acting. I am going to skip over every single one of those *massas* like Luigi jumping over turtle shells in *Mario Bros.*

3. "Go without me"? *Go without me* is something I tell my friends when they want to go to the Jersey Shore for the weekend. It is the *most* cazsh (short for *casual*) way to decline an invitation for a low-stakes situation. Slavery is the opposite of cazsh, so someone

re-upping for more slavery real chill, like it's a T-Mobile cell phone contract, is insane in the membrane.

4a. You're telling me that Slave doesn't even want to sleep on the decision? Even take half an hour to think this through, which is *still* less time than it took for me to come up with my Instagram handle? I'm sorry, but no slave should be treating the concept of freedom as casually as the way I blow off reading the Terms and Agreements page on iTunes so I can buy old Boyz II Men songs ASAP.

4b. Does she not have any slave friends she can run this conundrum by? We have all experienced being blinded by the nookie/dickmatized, so I am willing to suspend disbelief just to entertain that. Yet I cannot and will not accept that Slave doesn't want to Wingdings, Wingdings, Wingdings with any of the other slaves, who undoubtedly will be like, "You need to love yourself and leave." I mean, I've told my friends that even for low-stakes situations when they're drunk-texting me from a Carl's Jr. about a $50 food order they're about to make.

5. No slave is ever, ever, *ever* going to say yes to more slavery. There are no circumstances in which that would even make sense. Slavery is nothing but an endless cycle of physical abuse, rape, dehumanization, and mental anguish, so pretending as though turning down freedom is the same as someone turning down a job to work at the *Chicago Tribune* to stay in Bumblefuck, Iowa, with their boo is laughable.

6. Just so we're all clear. The Slave and Slave Owner Daughter are not going to live happily ever after. The happy ending here is that Slave is still going to be a slave, who can also sneak nookie in a linen closet with her white bae from time to time. I mean, it's not like the Slave Owner is going to sit down with his daughter and go, "OK, wow. So you're a lesbian. You're in an interracial relationship. You're sleeping with the hired help. Cool, cool, cool. Congrats on that," and then go back to being all rich, white, and evil. These two ladies are not going to be in a fair and equal relationship, and I resent the fact that the play is perpetuating an idea that the love of a white woman is more valuable than a black person's freedom. Talk about putting white people on a pedestal.

When we finished reading the play, it was dead silent in the room. Though I wanted to react by yelling, "This play is deep-fried in ignorance," I instead chose to do the whole angry black woman "measure twice, cut once" method. The first step: Over-analyze what you are thinking by weighing the pros and cons of saying your truth to someone who might not want to hear it. What were the pros? Standing up for black people and letting Rebecca know that this might be offensive to audiences. The cons? Telling her that what she wrote needed to be changed drastically would annoy her and, oh yeah, talking about the complexities of slavery within the confines of a short feedback session is uncomfortable and nearly impossible to do. *Still, this play is kind of fucked up,* I thought. So, I decided to forge ahead to the next step of the "measure twice, cut once" method.

Step two: Assess your surroundings. Done. Nothing but white people and me. Yowza. I knew that my surroundings raised the stakes, but since this classroom had always been a safe space for us to test out new ideas and give objective feedback, I gave myself the green light to proceed to the final stage.

Step three: Speak once (in a very non-threatening manner, of course). Duh. I know how to do that. My mom is an accountant and my dad is in real estate, so they are experts in talking in a way that gets work done and closes deals. They didn't raise no fool.

"Well, since I'm the only black person in the room, I

guess I'll go first," I began. "I don't think it really makes any sense that a slave would choose to remain in slavery because she fell in love with her slave owner's daughter."

"Well, it's a story about love conquering all," Rebecca responded.

Whoa, I thought, *she's not supposed to talk. It's the number one rule of workshopping. I did not plan for this.* You ever see a door at work that you're not supposed to open, but there's a little part of you that goes, *Well, what if you did*? So you do and then nothing bad happens? It's just the room with electric wires and a generator and you're like, *That's it*? and then Kanye-shrug all the way back to your cubicle? Well, that's what happened here. We all knew it was a no-no for the writer whose work was being discussed to speak, so none of us dared to do it. But then Rebecca did and... the world didn't stop. She simply spoke, and then it was my turn to speak. Like any other conversation. Oh. This threw me for a loop.

"But it's slavery."

"Yeah, but this is a brave story about two women defying the odds to be together."

"But the white woman is not sacrificing anything and the black lady is giving up everything. She's choosing *slavery*. No one would choose slavery." And with that the non-threatening speaking manner turned into a low-key version of John McEnroe's "You can't be serious!" I didn't raise my voice, but my tone was definitely one of incredulousness. I couldn't believe I was being forced into a situation where I had to explain that slavery is not a choice anyone makes.

The classroom was tense, like they were watching a ping-pong match between us. I don't remember much else of what was said, as I was juggling all sorts of emotions. I was upset, yet trying to make it seem that I was totally fine. I also worried about Rebecca's feelings because even though she was completely misguided, I related to her as a writer and knew how tough it was to hear the flaws in your work and not take it personally. More than anything, I was very aware that if I made one wrong step, this situation was going to turn ugly and we were headed for angry black woman territory.

What seemed like hours later, the professor stepped in to open up the room for more discussion. Thank Black Jesus, aka Gayle King's wig collection. Some other classmates chimed in and gently said that maybe slavery was not the best setting for her story, and Rebecca got visibly upset. After a few comments, she interrupted.

"I feel like I'm being picked on." Her voice trembled as she stared at me. Even though other people essentially said the same things I said, *I* was apparently the problem. She held the stare so everyone in class could see she was looking straight at me. "It's not fair." Tears welled up in her eyes. "You didn't even try to see what this play was trying to do. You just saw slavery and made up your mind about it and now you're picking on me." Never once did she break eye contact with me as the tears flowed. The message was loud and clear not only to me but to everyone in the room: *Phoebe is a bully. She is a mean black person. She is an angry black lady who made the white girl cry. She is a living stereotype.*

I didn't say anything back; I didn't know what to say because all I could think was *Oh, no. I made the white girl cry. I made the white girl cry. You're not supposed to do that. What is everyone going to think?* You see, I've spent my life learning that I am, at all costs, supposed to care more for a white person's feelings than my own. That if I hurt them or they decide that I have hurt them, that I am to feel guilty. And even in this situation, when it was so abundantly clear that I was not in the wrong for objecting to the romanticizing of slavery, for someone using the hundreds of years of pain and misery for my people as the backdrop for a love story, I was still being painted with the angry black woman brush. In that room, in that moment, I felt the most alone I had ever felt during my college experience.

Some of my fellow writers came up to me after class to reassure me that the points I made were valid. But what they said didn't matter. There was no one in the room who looked like me, who would truly understand what I was going through, who would know how embarrassed I felt. How shocked I was that her crying was more important than my having to sit through and participate in what essentially was a mockery of slavery. How disheartened I was that in 2006, it seemed that the whole messiness of slavery and race could be seen as just a problem for me and my people to untangle ourselves. How desperately I needed a look that could tell me, "Don't worry what the white people are going to think."

I don't know about other black people, but that Greek chorus of "But what will the white people think?" has been a constant in my brain for much of my life. "Man, I truly am going to be late, not because of CPT but because of traffic. But what will the white people think?" "I really want to order certain food off this menu at dinner. But what will the white people think?" "I want to speak out about some injustice I just witnessed. But what will the white people think? That I'm a troublemaker? Guess I should keep my mouth shut." Do you know the amount of minutes, hours, days, weeks, months, *years* that have been wasted second-guessing each and every behavior because I was wary of how I was going to reinforce or dismantle certain stereotypes? How often I shut my mouth and bit my tongue to avoid the "angry black woman" label? How draining it is to constantly scrutinize and edit all your actions before making them? That's not truly being alive; that's living on someone else's terms. And it sucks. But when you feel like that is your only viable option because the alternative—being even more misunderstood than you already are by society—is unbearable, what do you do? You cope with it until you figure out a plan. And for me, I found some relief through humor.

I'm not the first to claim this, but finding humor through shitty situations is the genesis of many comedians' careers. Whether it's being funny to make home life tolerable, or using wisecracks to win friends like I did way back in middle and high school, we all learn pretty early on that comedy is our mode of survival. Some people have their looks or athleticism or book smarts; we comics have our yuk yuks. It's our get-out-of-jail-free card. I mean, if I expressed my hurt in a clever, joking manner, no one can take offense then, right? No one can call you an angry black woman if we're all laughing, right? That was the tactic I took in my senior thesis class after the Rebecca incident. I made sure to diffuse with humor. When reading other friend's writing, I would pepper my feedback with jokes before giving my feedback. If a guy said something douchey to me, I would smooth it over with a quippy one-liner. If I had a disagreement with my goth roommate who would leave her Tamagotchi pet behind when she was gone for days at a time partying, which then forced me to "feed" and "play" with it, I would tease her about how she was an absentee parent out of an after-school special. And, sure, the teasing and joking made it so no one ever truly got mad at me, but it also prevented me from fully expressing myself.

Being on the charm offensive all the time will win you friends and help avoid conflicts, but it also leaves you feeling stifled and exhausted. At least that was the case with me. Trying to make sure everyone else was feeling OK was taxing, and it made me feel dishonest because I was sugarcoating everything I was saying. I felt like I wasn't being me but a version of me that was as non-threatening and inoffensive as possible. But that's the thing. Being true to oneself shouldn't be considered threatening. And it certainly isn't with white dudes when they speak up, so why was it with me? Oh, yes, the ole angry black woman thing. Hmm. *OK, well, I can let that stereotype dictate my life or I can live my life*, I thought. So I eventually chose the latter, with a sprinkling of comedy, of course.

When I started doing stand-up eight years ago, I found a confidence in myself that I didn't have. If I can stand onstage for twenty minutes at a time and command an audience with ease, then there is no reason I should be concerned about speaking up offstage. Slowly, I've become fearless in conversation and social media and have realized that I could slip my real opinions in about certain things among the jokes. Now, that doesn't mean that *everyone* loves this about me. I've gotten e-mails and messages claiming that I'm creating drama when it comes to race and gender issues. That I should just be happy with the way things are because I have Facebook, so how hard can my life as a black woman be? That I'm nothing but a thug, a whore, a cunt, and an animal. That I am just supposed to shut up and not make anyone feel bad about their careless and reckless behavior. That if I offer these opinions with no apologies and not enough J/Ks, then clearly I'm an "angry black woman." You know what? They can go ahead and think that. Really. I'm fine with it. You hear that? There's no Greek chorus in my head going, *But what will the white people think?* anymore. I am no longer concerned with that. What matters is that I *know* who I am. I'm a black person who happens to be a woman, and who happens to be a skosh angry from time to time about some pretty crappy things, and who happens to make some jokes when talking about those things I'm a skosh angry about. Ya know, a gahtdamn human being. So take that, Sapphire.

People, Places, and Things That Need to Do Better

~

If you haven't been able to tell by now, tons of stuff in this crazy, crazy world really burns my toast, so I want to, for once and for all, turn my attention to the people, places, and things that need to pull a Channing Tatum and *Step Up*. OK, OK. I know that if I'm going to name-check anything in Tatum's canon, it should be the Magic Mike series, which was clearly designed to create world peace/cure all diseases/ prove to the world that air humping is a lost art right up there with speaking Aramaic or prank calling in the days before caller ID. But this essay is for the purpose of reading, not sending you down a rabbit hole of GIFs and YouTube vids of Tatum the shirtless wonder. We don't have time for that because there is a more important item at hand: calling out all the stuff in culture that is "*turrible*," as Charles Barkley would say. Since I'm about to offer up some tough love, I don't want any of the following people, places, and things to feel like they're being attacked. I'm not perfect, so I'm happy to turn the spotlight on myself first. Examine some of my own flaws. For instance:

I am the worst at remembering names, which is probably due to the fact that I have a ton of useless information in my head. For instance, did you know that on the show *Roseanne*, Becky was played by two different actresses—Lecy Goranson, aka the OG Becky, and then Sarah Chalke pre–*Scrubs* fame? Or that an American urologist bought Napoleon's penis for $40,000 at auction? You see, both these tidbits are very important and must be remembered forever, so unfortunately, there's no way I can make room to remember the name of, say, the production company executive that I had lunch with yesterday. Ugh, basically, my brain is an iPhone that doesn't have enough storage on it anymore because I used it all up to take poorly lit photos of omelets.

I'm also terrible at buying cards. Every year around Mother's Day, I think to myself, *Mama Robinson deserves to receive the best card from her loving daughter*. And every year, without fail, I wait until the last minute and then all the Mahogany and In Rhythm brands of Hallmark cards are sold out. All I'm left with is a bunch of white-people cards, where I have to color in the faces with a brown magic marker and write some Maya Angelou–sounding shit on the inside to offset the fact that the cover shows a *Brady Bunch*–looking blond girl in cuffed overalls who's skipping rocks across a lake. My mom certainly deserves better than that.

Hm. I wish I had some juicier stuff to share about myself. The truth is, I'm a pretty low-key person. I'm not hiding anything maj. Just your run-of-the-mill stuff like mentally spiraling into despair over my career or love life to the point where I lay in bed for hours crying as I feed myself milk chocolate–covered graham crackers. Is that relatable? Enough to make you feel a little sad for me? Maybe make it a little easier for you to swallow the fact that I'm going to start calling people out? Alright, good. Now that's off my chest, I'm ready to tell everybody and everything else to "Do better, y'all!" First up…

1. The NFL and Its Treatment of Women

Y'all, the NFL is about as American as apple pie, fireworks, and pretending that only the Olympic events we're good at are the ones that matter. And since I was born in the Midwest of 'Murica, it's pretty much my destiny and duty to be a lifelong football fan. There's just one problem. The NFL's relationship with women is *bad*. Like final season of *Dexter* bad. This is hugely disappointing because female sports fans want to be the Bonnie to the league's Clyde (the Bey and Jay edition, obviously), the Scully to its Mulder, the Harold to its Kumar. In other words, women are ride-or-die for the NFL, yet the sport doesn't seem to care how poorly its players treat women.

Of course, there's an argument to be made that the NFL doesn't even care about its players a whole heck of a lot either, considering its attempts to suppress Dr. Bennet

Omalu's research on the brain damage (chronic traumatic encephalopathy, aka CTE) caused by football-related head trauma. While it is certainly problematic that the league disregards the health and safety of its players, let's set that aside for the moment. Players are now aware of CTE and have known for quite some time that footballers, on average, have a shorter life expectancy than other athletes, so if they decide to keep playing the sport, they are doing so with full knowledge of the risks. But the women who were abused or sexually assaulted by NFL players? They never signed up for that, and the fact that the NFL consistently turns a blind eye to this problem is deeply disheartening and disturbing.

In case you need a refresher on some of these offenders, allow me to do a roll call: Baltimore Ravens' Ray Rice. Former Cleveland Browns' player Johnny Manziel. Dallas Cowboys' Greg Hardy. Tampa Buccaneers' Jameis Winston. Pittsburgh Steelers' Ben Roethlisberger. Chicago Bears' Santonio Holmes. San Francisco 49ers' Ahmad Brooks. Philadelphia Eagles' Jordan Hicks. Buffalo Bills' Richie Incognito. NY Jets' Brandon Marshall. These are just a *handful* of players who have been accused of sexual and/or physical abuse. In 2015, there were forty-four active players who were accused of some sort of assault against women. And except for Ray Rice and Johnny Manziel, none of these men have faced real consequences, outside of a few instances of game suspensions and five-figure fines. Winston was still drafted number one overall in the NFL draft, despite the civil suit that his alleged rape victim filed against him and there being overwhelming evidence pointing to how Florida police officers on the case intentionally bungled the investigation from beginning to end to protect the star player. Hardy continued to start for the Cowboys even after Deadspin.com published photos of his battered and bruised ex-girlfriend after he assaulted and threatened to kill her. (The team owner, Jerry Jones, stated that he wasn't aware of Hardy's domestic violence until *after* he signed the corner-back to the team, so, whoops guess it's too late for Hardy to be properly reprimanded?) And then there's Roethlisberger, who has been celebrated as a hero of the game and is bound for the Hall of Fame, despite the allegations that he raped two women between 2009 and 2010. I mean… WUT?

How is that possible? How can we time and time again look the other way because these dudes are good at throwing pigskin on a well-manicured field? I mean, we're totally fine with letting these dudes off the hook, but we can't do the same for other people who are living far more innocent lives. To put this in perspective, we live in a world where Jennifer Aniston has gotten remarried and, like a dope-ass Jamaican lady, has multiple jobs, including acting and selling shea butter lotion and water, yet people are *still* talking about how Brad Pitt left her for Angelina Jolie. But when it comes to sexual misconduct, it seems everyone in the NFL and the media has amnesia? WHAT. DA. FUQ. How is a league that claims to be looking out for women via their annual highly popular and profitable breast cancer awareness campaign (which has also come under fire for the alleged discrepancy in how much of the profits from the merchandise actually goes to breast cancer research) be so tone-deaf and ineffectual in combating what is clearly a shameful problem? It is especially repugnant considering women make up a sizable portion of their viewing audience. According to Forbes.com, 45 percent of all NFL fans are women. Wow. Even a big football fan such as myself didn't know that before hitting the Google. Since so many ladies watch this pastime, where are the receipts from the league proving that they give a damn about the group that comprises almost half its fan base? I'm looking underneath my couch, inside my junk drawers, on top of my desk, NFL, but I can't find them. In fact, it seems the only woman-friendly move that the NFL has made in the past few years is to sell jerseys that are more figure-flattering for women. Don't get me wrong. I totes appreciate the attire, but it's very little consolation for the continual abuse.

So why do players continue to go unchecked after being accused of committing such heinous acts? Is it a matter of money, and the NFL not wanting to reprimand star players who bring fans to the sport? Is it that the NFL is misogynistic and simply doesn't care about women despite the spending power they yield? Is it that society doesn't take domestic violence and sexual assault seriously until it's too late or unless the victim is someone high profile and/or more popular than the assailant (e.g., Rihanna and Tina Turner)? Sadly, I believe it's a combination of all of the above. While the reasons may not be easily defined, we can say for damn sure that the NFL can do better. If they can sit back year after a year while women attend NFL games and buy NFL merchandise in record numbers, then the league can certainly protect the victims of domestic violence and sexual assault.

Simply put, the league's lack of support for women makes it mighty hard for me to remain a fan. It also makes it hard for me to want to teach my niece, who is growing up in the Midwest just like I did, to love the game. All I want is for the NFL to show that our well-being matters to them, that they see us as human beings who should be protected. Love us like we love them. Well, except the Pittsburgh Steelers, who are the bitter rivals of my ne'er-do-well Cleveland Browns. I gots nothin' but hate for the Steelers.

2. Barneys and Any Other Store That Makes Shopping Unpleasant for People of Color

Y'all, I used to think that buying things online was for shopaholics who were ashamed of their addiction and for people on shows like TLC's *I Weigh a Fuck Ton, So I Can't Get Up from This Couch (And Yes, "Fuck Ton" Is a Legit Unit of Measurement)*. I mean, why would you shop at home when you can go into a store and actually touch, smell, and fall in love with the thing you are about to buy? Oh, riiiiiiiight, because if you're a person of color, there's a strong chance that an innocent shopping experience can turn into "a very special episode" on a TGIF sitcom. Take, for example, the experience of Kayla Phillips and Trayon Christian. These two made national headlines in 2013 when they were accused of fraud after making expensive purchases at the upscale Barneys. Shortly after these embarrassing confrontations came to light, and after massive blowback from the public, the upscale retailer agreed to pay a settlement, including a $525,000 fine, as well as hire an independent anti-profiling consultant for two years, so as to prevent any more of these instances. While it's great that Barneys owned up to their racist and discriminatory behavior, when it boils down to it, this type of thing happens all the time. And it's not just exclusive to higher-end stores either. In 2013, bestselling author Roxane Gay was profiled at a Best Buy when a security guard did not believe the receipt documenting the items she purchased were indeed paid for... even though on the receipt *it showed that money was exchanged for these electronics*. Hell, employees at my local 99-cent store follow me around their establishment like we're reenacting a Benny Hill video. Except there's no laugh track, no zany music. Just a lot of irritation, questioning why the eff I even left the house that day if I'm just going to be hounded. Because this kind of mistreatment is a widespread issue, shopping is a somewhat stressful situation for me, and I'm sure many other POCs feel the same way. Whenever I go shopping, I become hyper-aware that I'm black, and thereby I'm hyper-aware of how employees will read my behavior. For example, I have enough experience shopping to know that when I dress down, I'll get shittier service, which explains why, on occasion, I've been known to be about one bow tie away from looking like Louis Farrakhan when I step into higher-end stores. Or it's as simple as when I go to a convenience store with a bottle of water already in my possession, I'll immediately find a security camera or an employee and make direct eye contact while taking a swig, so that they know I didn't steal the bottle. I make my hands visible at all times because I don't want any of the clerks to think I'm putting items in my pockets. The list goes on and on. It's an emotional experience, and it makes me want to shop at online stores exclusively so I don't have to deal with this bullshit. But that's not real-istic, and I'm a proactive person who will not settle for hiding. So here are some suggestions for improving poor retail behavior:

- Store employees, realize that your igno-rance has reached FEMA State of Emergency levels if the amount of time it takes me to get your attention is equal to or greater than the number of times I have to say *Beetlejuice* in order to summon him. Look, I understand. To survive working in retail, you must have a thousand-yard stare like you did three tours of Vietnam. But you don't need to pretend you're doing the Lord's work when you work at Uniqlo, folding sweaters while Huey Lewis and the News blares in the background. There is no reason why the entire first verse, chorus, second chorus, *and* bridge of "The Power of Love" plays before you acknowledge my presence.

- On the flip side, allow me to try on clothes in peace. Don't get me wrong. You can be attentive, but knocking on the dressing room door as if you're sending Morse code to an American ally in Ukraine is not helpful; it's meant to make your presence known, and as a result, I get nervous. So enough, 'kay?

- I mentioned it before, but it's worth repeating again: Stop following me and other POCs around the stores. It is a boneheaded move, and one literally proven to be ludicrous via statistics. As Jerome D. Williams, a professor and Prudential Chair in Business at Rutgers Business School, explains in his 2013 Huffington Post article entitled "A Message to Ponder on for Barney's, Macy's and the NYPD: Shoplifting Comes in All Sizes, Shapes, and Colors":

The reality is that non-minority shoppers account for most of the criminal activity. This is supported by data provided by the FBI's UCR database, which can be accessed online. Taking 2012 data, for example, the FBI data shows that approximately 70 percent of larceny/shoplifting arrestees are white. Our research suggests that whites don't frequently show up in shoplifting crime statistics to this degree because people aren't watching them. In fact, one could argue that whatever shoplifting statistics are reported in most cases have a built-in bias and are skewed upward. That's because the statistics actually are not really an indication of who's actually shoplifting. They are a reflection of who's getting caught, and that's a reflection of who's getting watched. It becomes a self-fulfilling prophecy.

Moral of the story: While you're spending all your time keeping an eye on me, some white dude just peaced out your store with an unpaid box of Froot Loops.

- Finally, be OK with your hand being near mine when handing me change after a purchase. Actually, be better than OK with it; I'm a gahtdamn human being. I'm not saying you have to hold my hand like you're playing a game of "Ring around the Rosie," but if the distance between our hands isn't less than the distance required between the faller and spotter during a trust-fall exercise at summer camp, then you're doing it wrong.

Look, I know I've been joking around a lot, but it's only to keep from being sad. These sorts of discriminatory things happen all the time, and most of the time, they don't make the newspaper. A lot of times, black people are just forced to suck it up and keep it moving. For instance, when a new organic food store opened in a (predominantly black) Brooklyn neighborhood I used to live in, I would say that for the *first year* of its existence, I was consistently followed around the store. Employees would pretend to be stacking loaves of bread when they were really checking to see if I was sneaking a jar of almond butter in my purse. Normally, I would be like, "Screw this place. I'll go somewhere else," but all the other stores in that neighborhood had garbage produce sections, so I sucked it up and put up with it. Eventually, they left me alone.

And that's absurd. It's absurd that was I judged from

the outset when I clearly make more money than all the damn employees up in that organic food store. It's absurd that after purchasing items from there the first time, it was not enough for the manager to realize I'm not a thief. It's absurd that there were some days I didn't go to that store because I just didn't have the strength to deal with being made to feel like a criminal in my own neighborhood. It's absurd that "shopping while being black" is a thing. It shouldn't be. Like all black people and other POCs, I just want to shop in peace, and until that happens, I guess I'll just be up in the crib, buying a fuck ton of clothes that I can't afford right now. But they will look super cute on me, so... Sorry, Suze Orman, for my poor financial decisions!

3. People Who Ask about My Relationship/ Family Status

Coming out of a long-term relationship has its down-sides. Your best friend who shared inside jokes with you is gone, you have to get used to not having a partner in crime when you want to go on vacation, ditch a lame party, or conquer a list of chores around the apartment. However, one of the worst downsides, by far, has to be friends and strangers I barely know wanting to get all up in my bidness about my personal life. When I say that I'm thirty-one, single, and don't have kids, don't respond with "You've got time," because I. CAN. SEE. YOUR. FACE. While your tone is as casual as the wardrobe at a Larry the Cable Guy concert, your face looks pained and concerned, like I just rolled into your son's christening and opened a Tupperware container full of tuna casserole.

4. White People Who Want There to Be a White History Month

You. Seriously. Need. To. Do. Better. Like, better yourself. Read a book.

5. Women Who Act Like Sexy Babies

When I think of the concept of sexy babies, my first two questions are: 1. How did this become a thing, and 2. Why did some women sign up for this way of being as easily as I signed up for LivingSocial newsletters? Sorry, I'm getting ahead of myself here. Some of you may not be familiar with the term *sexy baby*, so let me fill you in.

The world most recently saw a literal interpretation of this idea when grown-ass Miley Cyrus writhed around a crib and sucked on an oversized baby bottle suggestively in her "BB Talk" video. But, usually, sexy babies are more low-key than that. It's normally an underage girl walking around with juicy on the backside of her sweatpants, or an adult who is behaving submissively (speaking in a baby voice) to titillate. Either way, it's creepy and it sucks that this is a thing encouraged in people of the female persuasion. What about the dudes? No one tells them to behave like this. To be clear, I'm absolutely not about that sexy baby life, but if we're going to have lady sexy babies, there ought to be male sexy babies. There should be teenage boys who walk around with just got a handle on this whole wet-dream business on the backside of their sweatpants. Where are the men who trash-talk in a baby voice when playing *Grand Theft Auto*: "I'm going to shoot you wit mah widdle gun?" Turns out there aren't any *because it's gross*. So I say to women, you need to step it up and stop this nonsense. You're better, and you deserve better than this. Trust. Me.

And to the young'uns who are going, "Aren't you a feminist? Why are you judging other women?" all I have to say is, "Because you're twenty-one and your face is serving *Dora the Explorer* realness, yet your clothing conveys that you know more about Frederick's of Hollywood than Frederick Douglass. So how could I *not* put on a doily and *Judge Judy* you?" But in all seriousness, the infantilization of women perpetuates inequality, and when that is conflated with sex, it's easier to reduce women to objects and strip them of the power they have over their bodies. I can't go for that, which is why I believe there are other, more positive things women should be encouraged to be.

How about "Adult Woman Who Prays She Will Gray as Elegantly as Bonnie Raitt Even Though She Knows She's Going to Look Like Cornel West"? Or "Lady Who Can Do the Duet Song 'It Wasn't Me' Expertly by Herself"? Or "Grown-Ass Woman Who Is about Her

Business"? These are all amazing options, and I plan on being all these things before I die. Women who play sexy babies, I encourage you to join me.

6. The Waffle Houses in Breaux Bridge, Louisiana

You guys don't have *any* fruit on your menu, but you have thirty different waffle options? This, my friends, is what they call in the biz a "winter is coming" situation. My apologies to my digestive system because over the next couple of days, I'm about to eat. All. Dem. Waffles. But for serious, the Waffle Houses of Breaux Bridge. It would not kill y'all to have at least one piece of fruit that would've made Eve's defiant ass go, "Oooh, I'mma eat me some of this. Sorry not sorry, God."

7. Catcallers

PSA: Catcalling me by stating that you would let *me* do *your* laundry is just a roundabout way of saying, "Hello there, beautiful stranger! Just thought I'd let you know that I'm giving myself a HJ tonight!" Seriously, catcallers, knock it off. Stop assaulting me with comments about what domestic stuff I can do for you, stop demanding that I smile, especially when you see me carrying something heavy, stop berating me if I reject your advances, and enough with following me because I didn't respond to your yelling. I know you think you're being persistent like in all those rom coms where the basic plot is "women have bird brains, so it's up to men to charmingly badger ladies until they want to sheath your penis in their vajeen the way Jaime Lannister does his sword into his scabbard." But behaving as if you know what's best for a woman, especially one you haven't met, as if she has no agency of her own, is not cute. It's creepy and it's giving us serious *Law & Order: SVU* vibes. If you really do want to compliment a woman, then find a more creative way to do it than yelling comments at her the way Spike Lee does at the New York Knicks during a play-off game.

8. Stylists

Being a stand-up comedian/writer/actress has fun perks, like working with my comedy heroes (ahem, Janeane Garofalo), receiving free clothes from a company (thanks a mil, BB Dakota), and feeling that indescribable rush that happens when I tell a new joke and a bunch of strangers laugh till tears come out their eyes. But there's one perk that I never predicted I would enjoy, and that is working with stylists on photoshoots.

Despite the fact that I'm not a girly girl or a huge fashion maven, I love working with stylists. A lot. We watch the same TV shows, like the same music (anything Top 40), and share war stories about the trifling dudes we have dated. Now, with that out of the way, let me get down to the real. I have only one complaint about stylists. They'll ask for my measurements in advance of me showing up to a shoot, but nine times out of ten, when I arrive, they end up handing me size two/four clothing, as if the measurements I provided them had Choose-Your-Own-Adventure vibes where every ending is Zoe Saldana. I am not Zoe Saldana. I will never be Zoe Saldana. I am Phoebe Robinson, stylists, and I need y'all to hear me when I tell you things like my hip measurements because my hips don't lie. They are telling the truest truth when they say, "Yo, I can be on Food Network because these jeans this stylist has me in is turning me into some Grade A muffin tops."

Whew! This is quite a list, in which all of the things on it are of high priority. OK, getting Waffle House to add a fruit cup to the menu mayyyy not be as urgent as the NFL valuing women, but still, I can't help but feel passionate about each of these topics. Regardless, I hope what I've written here will help each of these people, places, or things reconsider how they've been operating and strive to make some sort of change. And if that change takes time, that's fine. Nothing good happens overnight. I mean, I did just give my mom a birthday card, and next to the illustration of the white lady on the card, I drew an arrow and wrote: "This is you except you're black." So, yeah, we all have some growing to do. So let's try and get better together. Cool?

Letters to Olivia

Well, we've reached the end of this book. Normally, I'd be like, "Byyyyyyyyye," and go back to updating my nail-art Pinterest page—#ImBasic—but not today. Today, I'm ending this book like how my parents do phone calls: by saying good-bye and then talking for another thirty minutes. (Mom and Dad, I'm teasing! I love our long chats.) Anyway, dear readers, it turns out there's still a few more things I have to explain, and I have to explain them to my all-time favorite person: my two-and-a-half-year-old biracial niece, Olivia.

Olivia is what they call in the biz "a Toyota Prius." In other words, she's a hybrid—half-black and half-white. She's new to this whole living thing, and she's got a lot to learn. And she seems to be a quick study. She's already got walking, laughing, and telling people to read to her on lock. Plus, she has that awesome baby scent that makes her smell like everything that's good and right in the world. Clearly, life has been nothing but a parade of awesomeness. But she's going to get older and encounter her fair share of ding-dongs who are going to make life difficult for her because she's a woman. Meaning she's not going to be paid as much as her male counterparts in the workplace, she's going to be cat-called by men for many of her teenage and adult years, and she will have to pay a "luxury" tax for menstrual products because forty states including New York, Ohio, and California deem those products as unnecessary. Yeah. No. I'm going to have to pull a Sam Waterston on the OG *Law & Order* and object to this lunacy. Spending five to seven days of every month preventing my undies from turning into Jackson Pollock paintings is not a luxury, so to those forty states, I say this: My tamp-tamps are as gahtdamn necessary as the black castor oil Jermaine Jackson uses to paint the hairline on his forehead.

Anyway, I can go on and on listing all the inconveniences and discriminatory things that women experience, but then this essay would be five hundred pages long, and I know you don't want to read that. Besides, gender discrimination is not the only thing Livvie will have to contend with. Being biracial comes with its own unique set of concerns. For instance, because her racial identity is more complex, some white people and black people will make her feel as though she doesn't belong in either group. Subsequently, the way she is treated will be markedly different than how either of her parents are treated. And that treatment will help shape her in different ways that none of us in the family will be able to predict. This all awaits my little cinnamon angel, and so I want to prepare her for this as much as possible.

And while I'm certain that her parents, PJ and Liz, are going to do a phenomenal job raising her, their hands are obviously very, very full, teaching her to take care of herself, sharing their appreciation for the value of a dollar, and that whole not letting her die thing, so they might forget to mention other equally important nuggets such as making sure she has the video of DMX singing "Rudolph, the Red-Nosed Reindeer" downloaded on her phone so that bundle of joy is at her fingertips at all times. If I know my brother and my sister-in-law as well as I think I do, PJ and Liz are going to be so focused on making sure Olivia becomes a phenomenal citizen that the DMX tip and other such gems might fall through the cracks. Not on my watch!

So that's why I'm taking the knowledge I've accumulated over the past thirty-one years and paying it forward to Olivia in a series of letters... which is a mode of communication that's super obsolete and will make me less cool in her eyes when she gets older. Heck, she might even be like, "What is a letter? People just blink three times to send message to each other in this day and age." Well, Olivia, I'm in the mood to kick it old school, so I'm typing it up and putting it in this book so your parents can let you read it when you are an appropriate age. If you're hankering for some Auntie Phoebe knowledge now, then you can have them read these letters to you "radio edit" style, and they can omit any mentions of peens and vajeens and *F*-bombs. So without further ado, enjoy. And if, at any point, I'm turning into *my* parents and going on and on, feel free to imitate Andre 3000 in "Hey Ya!" by going, "Alright, alright, alright, alright, alright, alright, alright, alright, alright, alright, alright, alright, alright, alright, alright, alright" and close the book.

Letter #1: Lisa Bonet Is Bae. Queen. Jesus.

Dear Olivia,

If you only take one thing away from these series of letters that I'm writing you, let it be the following: Actress Lisa Bonet is Bae. Queen. Jesus. This might seem like quite the exaggeration, but I assure you it is not. It's very important that as a person of color, you find people in media who have the same background as you so you know that you belong. And in my eyes, Lisa Michelle Bonet is the dopest, chillest, coolest, most badass, most interesting, and most gorgeous half-black chick in all the land. If I ever get the chance to be in the same room as her, I will Tebow before her and offer my left kidney should she ever need it. OK. I should probably back up because I understand that Bonet is before your time, Olivia. Some other biracial lady is probably your main shero right now, but I'm telling you to put her aside, because Bonet is the OG.

Bonet is best known for playing Denise, the eldest daughter on *The Cosby Show*. I don't want to say too much about the show because of Bill Cosby (Cringe alert! Ask your parents about him later), but I will tell you that it was one of my favorite shows as a kid. On it, Bonet was funny and intelligent, and she pulled off the perfect blend of masculine/ feminine clothes, like a biracial Diane Keaton. Plus, every guy wanted to date her, even when she had braces! I wished I could be like her when I was a teenager, not only for the example her character set on the show, but for how she lived her life in the spotlight, too. While she may have played by the rules on *The Cosby Show,* she went on to show the world that she lives by the motto of "I'mma do me." Bonet took control over her career in a big way, even when she was acting on *The Cosby Show*. She straight up defied Bill, who wanted everyone in the cast to have a squeaky clean image, by acting in the X-rated movie *Angel Heart*. She also refused to play the Hollywood game by rocking dreadlocks, no matter what kind of character she portrayed. And best of all, she was adamant about keeping her private life private, never playing into the celebrity fame game like others in her generation. In other words, she became, for me, the ultimate symbol of giving zero damns. And for this, she is Bae. Queen. Jesus.

So yes, I want you to let Bonet be your guiding light, but that doesn't mean she should be the only inspiration you have. Obviously, your parents are another light, and hopefully I am one, too. But there should be other biracial peeps you can look to as inspiration. That's why I've created this very handy list featuring some of the most important half-black people that you ought to know.

Mariah Carey: She writes her own songs, can hit notes that only Clifford the Big Red Dog can hear, and dated Nick Cannon of *Drumline* fame. We all thought that was going to be a "LOL, J/K, BRB" situation, but then they were married for seven years and had two kids before getting divorced. Moral of the story: One person's *Deuce Bigelow: Male Gigolo* is another's *Citizen Kane*.

Barack Obama: Uh, hello, he became the first half-black president. Plus, one time, when he was discussing the state of race in this country on a podcast, he said *nigger* and everyone freaked the hell out. Like "ripping their hair out, leaving only some stringy Gollum-like strands" freak out. Obama clearly knows how to keep it spicy.

Halle Berry: Talented and a number one stunner. It's not fair. Also not fair? That I've spent a considerable portion of my adult life unsuccessfully trying to emulate the scene from *Die Another Day,* in which Berry seductively struts out of the ocean. You will fail at attempting this, too, and that's OK. Stuff like that will keep you grounded.

Jude Law: LOL. J/K. I just included him here because when I Googled "famous biracial celebrities," Law popped up in the search results. Google is ignorant sometimes. That said, he is mad cute, so he's on this list.

Malcolm Gladwell: He has written many important books that you should definitely read (*Outliers* is my fav, BTdubs), and he's incredibly well respected. I once saw him at a restaurant in upstate New York and was like, *Oh shit, is that my uncle?* It was not. Point is, Gladwell kind of looks like he could be a member of any black person's family, and I think that's pretty cool.

Grace Colbert (biracial girl in Cheerios ads): This may seem ridiculous now, but in 2013, Cheerios released a thirty-second ad about a mixed family eating cereal, and the world panicked.

Sade: Sade is the *truth*. Everyone loves her music, and she's very potent in romantic situations. That's why you can't listen to Sade with just any guy or gal (I don't know your journey yet) because her songs seal the deal to Commitment Town. So unless you're certain you'd bone someone during the unsexiest of situations—*Good Morning America*'s George Stephanopoulos yammering in the background about pesticides harming America's produce—don't listen to Sade with this person.

Slash: IRL his name is Saul Hudson, and yet he still went on to play guitar in one of the best rock bands of the '90s (Guns N' Roses), was an animated character on *The Simpsons*, and continues to wear sunglasses all the time without anyone giving him shit for it. A fucking *SAUL* did all this, so you have no reason not to be a badass, Olivia.

Jennifer Beals: She was in *Flashdance* and *The L Word*. What more do you need?

Stacey Dash: She kind of sucks, but whenever I rewatch *Clueless*, I fall in love with her all over again. So check her out in that movie and skip anything she does on FOX News.

Tiger Woods: He was one of the greatest athletes in the world until his roving peen got the best of him and everyone learned he was a sex addict who continually cheated on his wife. Two takeaways here: 1. I think golf is hella boring, but if I discover you're naturally gifted at the sport, I'm becoming your manager so we can get rich, and 2. if you're having so much sex that you need to pull a Walter White and have multiple burner phones in order to juggle all your jump offs, maybe bone less?

Maya Rudolph: One of the funniest people on the planet. I mean, what is life without humor? If you can be a sliver as funny as her, then you'll be made in the shade. Also, one time, she was checking into a hotel as my buddy and I were checking out of it, and she started talking to us like we're friends. So I thought, *Are we friends?*

And she responded, *No, but I like your sunglasses, though.* Olivia, Maya Rudolph can read minds like she's Buffy the Vampire Slayer.

Prince: He began as a wunderkind, then morphed into a sexy provocateur, then became an elder statesman of music who influenced countless acts. He carried himself with the confidence of an auntie who thinks you ain't shit because your potato salad sucks. Essentially, he lived all the lives I would ever want to live. And when you are older, I will play you all his music and we will have the most epic and adorable auntie-niece dance party.

The Rock: He's hot and funny and has an adorable relationship with his dog. He's basically perfect. Even though I'm afraid he would snap my hips like a wishbone if we ever had sex, I would still give it the old college try so I can have his babies. Hmm, I guess you didn't need to know that about your aunt. And you can't un-know it. Sorry 'bout that.

Derek Jeter: He is a legendary Yankee and was a notoriously charming playboy. Stay away from dudes like him and date dudes named Saul. And I don't mean the Sauls that grow up to become Slashes. #Callback. I'm talking about Sauls that marinate in their Saulness and the most excitement of their life is when their new Blue Apron package arrives.

Bob Marley: He's a legend. Duh.

Well, Livvie, that's my guide to VIP biracial people. Hope you learned a lot and feel confident that you can take on the world! If you're ever lost or filled with doubt, just ask yourself, "What Would Lisa Bonet do," and you'll be all right, 'kay? She is, on the regs, sexin' on that hot Samoan dude from *Game of Thrones*, and before that, she was married to Lenny Kravitz and made the ultimate Blewish (black and Jewish) child in Zoë Kravitz. Bonet clearly knows what the hell she's doing, so follow her lead.

Love,
Auntie Phoebe

Letter #2: Throw (and Do Everything) Like a Girl

Dear Olivia,

Just so we're on the same page, I absolutely loathe when musicians give their GRAMMY acceptance speeches and say, "I just want to thank all my haters. Y'all are my motivators." Calm. Your. Tits. Rapper Dude. Stop taking yourself so seriously. You didn't invent anything; you're just really good at slant rhymes. Anyway, even though I'm so over the hater shout-out at award shows, there is one time I'm all for saying it. It's whenever, not *if*, but when, someone goes, "Olivia, you [insert a verb] like a girl." This will usually be said in jest, as if being what they consider the "lesser" sex is funny (*eww*) or as an insult so you'll feel bad about yourself (double *eww*). Either way, the underlying message is the same: Being a girl is quite possibly the worst

266

thing in the world, and anyone who is female should either be pitied or laughed at. Screw that!

Being a woman is not a horrible fate one is saddled with, and I resent the idea that half of the world's population is deemed, right out the gate, to be as pitiful as a pair of irregular JCPenney jeans on 80 percent discount. Sure, as I mentioned earlier, it sucks getting paid less than men, and being catcalled on the regular is nobody's idea of fun; but don't be mistaken, being a lady *is* amazing. Just look at your mom and consider the amount of things she does in a given day—working, cooking, balancing a checkbook, loving you and your dad, doing the "Single Ladies" dance from memory, gobbling up knowledge from books and newspapers, laughing at the BS society throws her way, and continuing to kill it. She is a great example of how women can kick ass. And there are *tons* of other dope things dub-X folks do. Take softball player Mo'Ne Davis. She was just *thirteen* years old when she could throw a seventy-mile-per-hour fastball. Or how Misty Copeland made ballet history when she became the first African-American woman to be made principal dancer at the American Ballet Theatre.

Or the fact that Emma Watson announced she is taking a hiatus from acting to solely devote her time to her work as a UN ambassador for her new feminist organization HeForShe, which encourages men to be involved in making gender equality a reality. The point is, women are clearly awesome, and you need to remember that, Olivia. That way, whenever someone tells you that you're doing XYZ like a girl, then you can whip out, "Thank you, hater, you're my motivator," and then go back to being XX chromosome AF.

In fact, *be XX chromosome AF* should be your life motto. It's mine, although it took me a while to figure that out. I've always been proud to be a woman, but I just needed a kick in the pants to truly take ownership over my "ladyship." That booty kick came when I was twenty-three, which is no coincidence because that is when I started doing stand-up comedy, a field that has become one of the great loves of my life. Despite my devotion to the art form, there's no denying that it is a very male-dominated world and one that discourages women from fully embracing those dub Xs.

Because the industry is so male-dominated, many female comics have to engage in hyper-masculine behavior in order to be taken seriously. It's present in everything, from how we're expected to talk about comedy to how we physically act when we perform. For example, when comics do well, we say we "killed," "murdered," "destroyed." When we have a terrible set, we say, we "ate a massive dick," "bombed so hard," "died." At shows, there's always an air of competition. Most of the time it's friendly competish, but still, the vibe is the same: On some level, we want to do so well that the next person cannot follow us. That they do horribly. That they dine on that giant sauseege we prepared for them. What I'm saying is that the comedy world oozes machismo. The most glaring evidence of this is the fact that 90 percent of shows have a mostly male lineup, with one or two spots designated for women. And since this is the norm, audiences have been conditioned to instinctually enjoy listening to anything about the male experience and to be somewhat resistant or hesitant to listen to stuff from a female perspective. In a lot of ways, it's almost as though anything outside the heteronormative male experience is deemed not worthy of discussion.

Case in point: I did a show recently and

said the word *vagina*, to which a man yelled out, "Oh, God!" Another time, a guy sitting in the front row turned beet red and literally covered his face à la Taylor Swift winning an award because he had to listen to me talking about the very real issue that afflicts women when they gain weight: Their down-there, lady-bit area also gains weight. Naturally, the women in the audience laughed those "This happened to me, too, girl" laughs, while the dudes were shocked and horrified. I'm sorry, if we can hear and *love* it when Louis C.K. jokes about letting his dog lick peanut butter off his peen, then everyone can get on board with me being like, "Yo, just so y'all know, women gaining weight in their vagina area during the course of a relationship is similar to those time-lapse videos of a soufflé rising in the oven." Whether or not I was funny when talking about my body wasn't even the issue. The real problem was that I dared to talk about my body in the first place, and that shocked the male crowd.

The point is this. Male comics, and the entertainment sphere in general, are encouraged and celebrated for discussing all things dude-related, especially if what they are talking about is their body. It's feels as though we live in a world in which everything seemingly comes back to the dong. Olivia, I once had a male comic, who went on stage after me, start his set by talking about how he would have sex with me. That's it. No humorous line of reasoning. No interesting commentary. Just some thought about how he would bone me. And people laughed. Not pity laughs, but belly laughs. Meanwhile, I was just watching this unfold, waiting for anything that resembled a joke. None came, yet he got rewarded by the audience for his Brick-Tamland-"I-love-lamp"-level rambling about what he and his penis would do to me. And just to be clear, this is not some one-off wacky situation. Every single female comedian has *multiple* stories about a comic or a heckler reducing her to a sexual object. She also has *multiple* stories about a time when she did feminist material or jokes about something from the female perspective, and the audience was like, "hard pass," as if it's too big of an ask for men to relate to something outside of themselves.

In no particular order, here are just a handful of warnings/gripes I've heard about lady comedians from men during my nine years of doing stand-up comedy:

- "Women shouldn't talk about periods because it's gross."

- "Women talk about relationships too much."

- "There can't be more than one woman on the lineup because then the audience will think this is some weird all-girl show and this is just a regular show."

- "We had a woman perform at this club last year and she didn't do too well, so we're cooling it on booking women for a while."

- "Women need to be pretty when they perform."

- "Why do some women wear makeup on stage? Comedy is not about looks."

-

- "Pretty women can't be funny."

- "Oh, that girl is funny. I wonder if she's a lesbian because lesbians are really the only funny women."

- "Women would get more spots on shows, but they don't ask for them."

- "I really hate when women ask for more spots on shows; it's so pushy."

- "No one wants to see a pregnant woman do stand-up because they're worried she's going to go into labor."

- "Women comedians get further in their careers if they're single or present themselves as single because then it gives male comics and industry people hope that they can fuck them."

- "Women get into comedy to find a boyfriend and not to be funny."

- "This girl's a prude because she doesn't bang any of the comics."

- "She has sex with *all* the comics."

And so on and so on. Now, I'm not looking for empathy here. None of these statements are things that I can't handle, but I think it's fair to say that in this day and age, the fact that these sorts of sexist comments are still routinely uttered is ludicrous. For women comedians to still be functioning

273

in a workplace that reminds them that the essence of who they are is not entirely welcome is mind-boggling. And furthermore, that the idea of owning who you are—dub Xs—and not shying away from it in your material is seen as a defiant, almost revolutionary act seems, well, a tad silly. Shouldn't it no longer be "shocking" to hear a woman talk about her body other than in a "self-deprecating, please like me" way? Unfortunately, Olivia, the answer is still no. Getting into the nitty-gritty of the XX chromosome AF life is still seen as alienating even though folks like Margaret Cho and Wanda Sykes have shown that female audiences crave having their life experiences reflected back at them for years. So much of comedy is about us all realizing, *Hey, maybe I'm not such a weirdo after all/Oh my God! You do that thing, too?/Holy crap, you just said everything I ever wanted to say, but didn't have the tools to do so*. The joy of seeing yourself in another is pertinent not just to stand-up comedy but to being alive.

Seeing women like Margaret Cho and Wanda Sykes and Janeane Garofalo share their experiences empowered me to forge ahead, full throttle, and celebrate every part of me that I'm supposed to deny in order to make it in this business. In every facet of my career and my life, I embrace my womanhood and talk about it constantly. And so do my lady friends, because we are on a mission to normalize our experiences. We do things like women, and we're proud of it. And I want you to be proud of it, Livvie.

It's important that you remember that, because throughout your life, people are going to imply that who you are is a worst-case scenario, or not interesting or worthy of discussion. It might be when you're playing catch with some boys at school and you don't throw the ball as far as they can. They'll laugh and say, "You throw like a girl." Or maybe you're in a foot race and they'll go, "You run like a girl." You might cry in public because your feelings were hurt or because you fell down or because life is really, really freakin' hard and you'll be told, "Ugh, you're such a girl." "What a crybaby." Perhaps you want to talk about uniquely female situations and boys will get grossed out and try to silence you. Instead of complying, Liv, lean into your "girlness." Throw it in people's faces that you are fully embracing everything they think is a flaw. Eat, cuss, laugh, feel, dance, fight, dress, think, love, and tell your story like a girl, which means do everything you intend to do with no regard for how people want you or expect you to behave. And if anyone has a problem with that, you can send them to me, and I'll handle it like a girl: write a long Tumblr blog post about this person and anonymously post it on Reddit, so it goes viral.

Love,
Auntie Phoebe

Letter #3: Your Parents Might Say They Didn't Name You after *Scandal*'s Olivia Pope, but They Totally Did

Dear Olivia,

If our aunt/niece bond is going to be as dope as the one that Rosemary had with her nephew George Clooney (No lie, that dated reference is my go-to one for this kind of familial relationship. Fuck, I'm old), then I have to be completely honest with you. For like 0.0000000000000001 second after you were born, I was mad at you. You see, your parents called me after you arrived and they told me they named you Olivia. Little did they know that name was at the top of the list of baby names I have for my future kids, if I have any. Other names include Jordan, Chloe... and that's it. So, I guess this is less a list and more like three names of ladies in a jankity girl group called Thrice as Nice. Still, I really loved *Olivia*, and when your parental units named you that, I guess the idea of *my* Olivia vanished. Gone was my daughter rocking the cutest braids, sometimes with beads at the end and other times like Moesha's. Bye-bye to my freakishly talented daughter knocking strangers' socks off. Adios to me cheering her on from the family-seating box while she competes at the US Open tennis tournament. Yeah, as I'm writing this out, I'm realizing that all these years I've just been daydreaming that I was Serena Williams's mom. The point is that my fantasy Olivia had to disappear so I could welcome the reality of the "you Olivia." So after being bummed—I swear it was for 0.0000000000000001 second—I was insanely happy because I get to be your *cool aunt who lives in New York*. I get all the fun of having a baby in my life with none of the responsibility. I get to send you presents and books and educational toys. I'm the one who gets to introduce you to cool music your parents don't know about. When they're tired, I'm still down for letting you use my body like a jungle gym and climb it for what seems like hours. We get to FaceTime and you put on a show, telling me all the new words you can say or what new stuffed animal best friends you have. Because I'm not around you every single day, I think it's funny when you fart. I mean, it's even kind of funny when you shart. Gross, but pretty funny. No matter what you do, I'm charmed and impressed by you. Because you're doing so many of these things for the first time and I get to see how you see everything. How it's all new and shiny and weird and funny and interesting. Seeing how you view the world makes me not the semi-jaded New Yorker I've become in a lot of ways. Seeing how you view the world makes me happy. Aah! A comedian expressing a genuine emotion and not following it with a joke. Full disclosure: That was really, really hard for me to do just then.

Since the full disclosure train is in effect, I might as well disclose something else to you. Your parents may not *admit* that they name you after *Scandal*'s Olivia Pope, but they totally did. In case you aren't aware, Olivia, in 2012, the highly addictive nighttime soap opera *Scandal* premiered on ABC and pretty much everyone dropped what they were doing to watch the show. Its main character, Olivia Pope, had it all: a killer wardrobe, her own lucrative business "fixing" the scandals of the Washington, DC, elite, and tons of #StruggleSex with the president of the United States (because in TV, the best way to illustrate an illicit couple in the throes of passion is to show them tugging at each other's clothes like kids on cow udders at a county fair). More important, her character was not someone's maid or the sassy best friend, as black women were so often depicted in pop culture. She was groundbreaking! So, as a result of *Scandal*'s insane popularity, more and more black people named their daughters Olivia. While I don't think Ms. Pope is the sole reason why your parents named you Olivia, the name must have gotten stuck in their brains. However, if we're going to be real, as exciting and cool as Pope is, she's kind of not the best role model; she constantly lies and covers up murders, but that's all right. There are some aspects about her that are great. She runs her own company, owns her own apartment, is extremely intelligent, and most important, she has the best lip quivers in the business.

While Kerry Washington seems to have toned down the LQs in later seasons, they were out in full force during seasons one and two and were used to signify when she was turned on, scared, or mad. It was during these early years of *Scandal* that I learned that in addition to having an IQ (mine is def twenty points lower due to my reality TV consumption) and an emotional quotient, everyone also possesses an LQQ, aka a lip quiver quotient. Unfortunately, my LQQ is still at minor-league status as it only happens when I'm singing along to Luther Vandross's woo-woo-wooing on his *Greatest Hits* album, but I'm working on it. And you should, too, because, in my opinion, Washington's lip quiver has officially dethroned Claire Danes's ugly crying in *Homeland* as the ultimate dramatic facial expression. So it only makes sense that you get the basics down if you're going to survive in this world.

Let's start with one that has a low degree of difficulty. It's basically the base on which all other lip quivers are built. I call it the "My Roommate and I Are Grocery Shopping for an Upcoming Hurricane and She Makes Me Remove the Two Six-Packs of San Pellegrino Limonata and the Lorna Doone Cookies from the Shopping Cart Because They Don't Count as Provisions." It's a subtle movement that lets people know you're disappointed but not emotionally broken. If you want to take it to the next level, I suggest the "I Was Chilling at Home Alone and Got Freaked Out Because I Heard a Strange Sound, but It Turns Out That Noise Was Just My Laptop Cord Sliding off My Desk" LQ. I like this one because it requires heavy breathing, so I count it as cardio on my Fitbit. Plus, this kind of lip quiver is versatile. You can use it in when a friend of yours is showing off her brand-new iPhone 7 when she knows doggone well that she owes you $37. Or when you're trying to get into an elevator and catch someone pressing the door-close button on you. It even works when you're insulted that a friend decides to round everyone up to leave because it's 2 a.m. and she's sick of doing karaoke. Basically, when in doubt, use this lip quiv.

Now that you know some of the basics and can serve Olivia Pope face, you must serve her fashion. This is tough to do because 1. her wardrobe is designer and very expensive, and

2. because a lot of it is white, it's super impractical in real life and after one day of walking the streets of Cleveland, your white duds will look like Daniel Day-Lewis's coal-miner character in *There Will Be Blood*. Might I suggest as an alternative to Pope's mostly white- and cream-colored wardrobe wearing whatever affordable and non-white clothes your mom buys you because you don't have a damn job? And when you do start working, if I find out you're spending your hard-earned money on a $1,000 white trench coat instead of putting it into a savings account, I will hide all your curl cream, so your hair will be frizzy for a week.

Speaking of hair, Pope's is incredible. When she's at work, it's sleek, shiny, and straight. When she's on vacation with a hot dude, it's effortlessly curly. Mimic that devotion to your mane. I know it's going to be tempting to let your beauty regimen go when you're on a trip. Don't fall for this temptation. I have before, and I wound up looking like the "Before" in a late-night weight-loss infomercial. Now, I'm not saying spend hours trying to look bomb AF when you visit your family during college break, but it won't kill you to do your hair in a recognizable style that's not "haystack in a barn." Besides, when you're on vacation, you'll never know who you're going to bump into, so you want to always be, as the kids says, "Stuntin' on these heauxes," aka looking fly.

About this whole looking-fly thing. Forget Pope's awesome hair and killer wardrobe. What truly makes her spectacular is her strut. Whether she is heading to an afternoon delight session with the president or marching toward a client who double-crossed her, her walk is fierce. If you can master this walk, it almost doesn't matter what else you got going on. Hell, you can look fly in a pair of pajamas while you're shopping at Sam's Club if you, like Olivia Pope, turn every walking opportunity into a Victoria's Secret fashion runway. This sounds harder than it actually is. It's really just a simple formula:

The leadership power walk of Harriet Tubman leading slaves through the Underground Railroad − H. Tubs's intensity + the chill vibes of Snoop Dogg after he just smoked a blunt. Meaning, each of your steps is purposeful, but you're not breaking a sweat. (Side note: When you are making Black History Month presentations in school, be sure to not include *Harriet Tubman* and *chill vibes* in the same sentence.)

So how are you feeling about all this, Livvie?

Good, I hope, because with these four Pope-isms—lip quivers, wardrobe, hair, and strut—you're well on your way to becoming the best Olivia you can be.

Love,
Auntie Phoebe

Letter #4: Don't Forget about Your White Side!

Dear Olivia,

I know I've been writing *a lot* about black-lady stuff, but we have to switch gears because you're half-white! And you should celebrate that, which is something society makes very difficult for mixed people. No matter what anyone says, I want you to remember and recognize your white side. Normally, this would be when I start giving you a bunch of advice about white life, but since I'm browner than a plate of *chicharrónes*, I'm bringing in guest writer John Hodgman, who is a fellow comedian-actor-author (check out his work on *The Daily Show*, please!), is quite the dandy (seriously, this guy always dresses like a businessman customer of Sweeney Todd's), and because he is a straight white dude, knows *everything* that's awesome about being white, including how people are impressed when he can spit the first sixteen bars of "Rapper's Delight." Ugh. Literally everyone knows that song, so color me unimpressed. Anyway, my friend John is super smart, hilarious, and you should trust everything he's about to tell you.

Dear Olivia,

My name is John Hodgman. I am a friend of your aunt Phoebe's. I'm on television sometimes.

A couple of years ago I had lunch with my friend Wyatt in Brooklyn, where we both live. After lunch I realized that there was an errand I had to run nearby. In this part of Brooklyn, there is a gourmet mayonnaise store, and I was commissioning a small run of special mayonnaise for an art project of mine[*].

---

[*] I was going to include a small jar of mayonnaise as part of a box set for a comedy performance DVD of mine. Along with the mayonnaise, the box would include a custom unisex fragrance I had made at great expense, as well as a silver flask marked urine, and a sample of my mustache hair. I can give you one if you like, Olivia. I have hundreds and hundreds of them in a warehouse in Massachusetts.

"Let me just go into the store and see how my private mayonnaise label is coming along," I said to Wyatt. And he said, "Sure." Wyatt is great.

Like a lot of new businesses in this part of Brooklyn, the gourmet mayonnaise shop was new, spare, and clean. Behind a glass window you could see into the mayonnaise lab so you could watch a man with a beard emulsify their perfected mayonnaise formula.

On a whiteboard behind him was the chemical notation of a certain molecule. I'm guessing a mayonnaise molecule.

At the front counter I spoke with the proprietress of the mayonnaise company, a charismatic woman with interesting tattoos and an interesting asymmetrical haircut who played in an art rock band at night. She showed me some sample labels for my custom run of mayonnaise, and I approved one. Before we left, we tried some of their new truffle-flavored mayonnaise.

And then we walked back out into the day of Brooklyn and what I considered to be a totally normal afternoon. But Wyatt stopped for a moment and blinked a couple of times thoughtfully. "I don't normally mention this kind of thing," he said, "but that was probably the whitest experience I ever had."

Now, Wyatt is black, and I am white, and his comment really took me by surprise. It took me by surprise in the way white people are constantly being taken by surprise. How could you consider something about my life being anything but totally ordinary and right? After all, I am a white person. Better than that, I am a straight white man, which for a long time in American culture equaled *default human*.

But that is changing. We are hurtling within this century toward the moment when those of us who are traditionally considered "white" will be a minority in this country. I say "traditionally considered white" because, of course, whiteness is made up. Like "black" or "Latino" or "Asian," or "Native American," "white" is just a clumsy catch-all for a whole bunch of distinct points of origin, ethnographic groupings, cultures, and histories.

But historically, "white" is a catch-all with one very important, toxic difference, in America especially: We're the good ones. The normal ones. The not *you*s. Even if we're poor, even if we're servants, even if we have no education, even if we're *Jewish*, we're the ones you can't enslave. We're the ones you can't beat without repercussion, who get to vote, and are protected by laws *no matter what.*

OK, again I'm mostly talking about white *men* here. But you get the idea: For a long time we were the culture that never had to explain itself, justify itself, account for itself. *Of course I'm* going to spend the day in an artisanal mayonnaise store. *Why should that even surprise you?*

Unfortunately, white culture is not just people with college degrees making white condiments in white rooms with whiteboards because they got seed money from probably white friends. In fact, a lot of white culture is pretty ugly. It's done harm to a lot of people. And it's ugly right now as I write this. At the time of this writing, Donald Trump seeks the Republican nomination supported largely by a bunch of angry white people who sense where history is going and DO NOT LIKE IT AT ALL and are therefore hoping that if they punch and shove enough brown people, it will fix it. Perhaps when you read this, Donald Trump will be president or maybe superking. But even if that happens, he shall pass. Time does not go backward.

But there are also some beautiful parts of your white heritage that are worth celebrating. I will leave aside global white culture because there is much to celebrate that I cannot properly lay claim to (David Bowie, Fry and Laurie, Kate Bush, Édith Piaf, the Enlightenment, Sex Pistols, and poutine), so I will constrain myself to the United States. And you are lucky, Olivia, that I am here to tell you about it because I was born in Massachusetts, birthplace of American caucasia, and there really is no mansplaining like white mansplaining.

There are some cultural institutions that most humans would agree are important or influential or inspiring or simply awesome—and in essence, undeniably white. Herewith, Olivia, a list off the top of my head based largely upon my own unique growing up and strange personal preferences. It's selective, I realize, so forgive me. White people have been paid to make culture for a long time!

The entire run of *Cheers;* Fleetwood Mac; They Might Be Giants; the Allman Brothers Band; both the Tom Waits and Bruce Springsteen versions of "Jersey Girl"; Charles and Ray Eames; *Grey Gardens* and all the work of the Maysles brothers; Metallica; Willie Nelson; E. B. White (it's right there in the name!); *The Simpsons*; Stephen King; *The*

Muppet Show; the stories of Raymond Carver; almost all public radio; *Twin Peaks*; Jonathan Coulton; *McSweeney's*; basketball *kind of* (it was invented by a white dude in Springfield, MA!) but *definitely* curling; the band Devo; the band the Pixies; at least the one song "Brandy" by Looking Glass; David Rees, whose favorite song that is; George Plimpton; *The Dick Cavett Show; Peanuts*, and its depressive spiritual successor, "The Gashlycrumb Tinies" by the genius Edward Gorey; *Moonrise Kingdom; Fargo;* the criminally forgotten film *Broadcast News;* Renaissance fairs; and absurdist fake trivia books such as *The Areas of My Expertise* by John Hodgman.

Olivia, you are very smart, so I don't need to explain to you why this list contains no white rappers or white jazz people, though there are geniuses in both camps.

I'd also set apart for special consideration the work of technically white but cultural, sexual, religious/ethnic outsiders like Andy Warhol; *The Godfather;* Divine; George Gershwin; almost every twentieth-century white American comedian; and on some level *every* white American woman. That's why you may have noticed I saved mention of such heroes as Laurie Anderson, Dolly Parton,

Rickie Lee Jones, Ursula K. Le Guin, Patsy Cline, Patti Smith, Elizabeth Gilbert, Merrill Garbus, Penelope Spheeris, Lois Lowry, Kelly Sue DeConnick, Lynda Barry, and so many others that I'm forgetting, I'm sure.

All women, to some degree, are excluded from the power and privilege grid that traditional "whiteness" connotes. Even Julia Child, who exuded a patrician kind of whiteness and lived in *Cambridge*, for god's sake, was a kind of revolutionary: encouraging women (and dudes) to be more adventurous, fearless, and worldly even if just in the kitchen. She was tall and commanding, she forced her husband to draw pictures of cow's stomachs for her, and she was a real-life spy. Damn.

Staying with public television for a moment, PBS of course deserves celebration for the early, radical diversity of *Sesame Street*. But let's be blunt: It's still pretty white, serving certainly in my childhood as the gateway to some of the finest and whitest world culture available, from *Doctor Who* to Monty Python. But, Olivia, you must know of the special feeling I have for Fred Rogers, a man who answered every joke about his status as perhaps the most clichéd white square dude with the kindest smile. Not only was *Mister Rogers' Neighborhood* devoted to showing people of different color, ability, and background, it was also devoted to showing kids that we are all equally scared, elated, anxious, grateful, sad, and most of all capable of managing this emotional complexity in time. And his insistence upon approaching the world, both real and make-believe, with openness, humility, and a desire to learn more than to teach has always been for me a model of white privilege–checking before there was a phrase for it. If you ever want a good cry, Olivia, find someone you love and sing to them a song by Fred Rogers that we should all know by heart called "It's You I Like."[*]

In this way, I think Mister Rogers is the humblest and most humane expression of what white culture has been able to do at its best: use the luxury of its reach, power, and pre-approval to expose and challenge injustice at a level that likely would have been automatically denied to non-white folks. There are the activists, of course, worth mentioning, too, when it comes to this type of social history, heroes like Gloria Steinem and Harvey Milk. Great political provocateurs

---

[*] Also, he was an advocate of local light rail and non-polluting public transportation throughout his life.

like Pete Seeger and Lenny Bruce.

And then there are the nerds: Rod Serling, the epitome of your '50s white dad with his suit and his smoke, who used creepy allegory to trick midcentury white TV owners to consider their complacency, xenophobia, and bigotry, as Gene Roddenberry would do on *Star Trek*, positing an empowered, multigender, multi-racial workplace like no big deal. Joe Shuster and Jerry Siegel created Superman, of course, the superimmigrant; Jack Kirby created the Hulk, the Thing, the X-Men, and a host more of Marvel's tortured weirdos and outsiders, and Stan Lee helped him. These early comics were *not* diverse—though Kirby and Lee introduced the first African-American super-hero, the Black Panther, in 1966—but they nonetheless were radical in American culture. They drew a blueprint not just for tolerance and inclusion of otherness, but for an *empow-ered* otherness that any young person could attach to, and which certainly did not exist in the rest of kids' entertainment in the '60s. And I'm glad to say that within the past five years or so, comics, embracing this legacy, have become perhaps the most diverse form of pop culture around.

And we can't forget about the *food* of white

culture, Olivia. What it suffers in blandness, white food makes up for in sheer salt and fat excess because we *are immortal and do not give a fuck!* Crème agnès sorel. Snowflake rolls lathered in butter. Creamed chipped beef on toast. Ten thousand varieties of mushroom-soupy Minnesota hot dishes, including the profoundly wrong tuna-noodle casserole. The noble, vinegary Taylor Pork Roll, and the coarse, menacing, truth-in-advertising pig-snout-and-cornmeal loaf called scrapple, the twin sausage totems of my mother's German-Irish family of Philadelphia. And yes: mayonnaise.

While both my parents went to college and gave birth to me, an only-child weirdo who ran home from high school each day to listen to *Fresh Air*, my mom grew up in working-class Philadelphia, the oldest of seven siblings. As mentioned above, there are many different kinds of white people, and while I was never unloved, it was clear from the moment I was old enough to grow a ponytail and wear a *Doctor Who* scarf (eleven years old) that my grandparents did not know what to make of me.

When we would visit, the ritual was the same. My grandfather would put out a spread on the kitchen table: six or eight kinds of lunch meat, including Pennsylvania esoterics like Lebanon bologna and souse; white and rye bread; pickles; two mustards; and mayonnaise. We would all sit around that kitchen table and construct our sandwiches and then eat those sandwiches in silence, because that is how white people show affection.

No matter my relatives' strangeness, I never felt more at home than at that table. I think of it frequently. And I still model my OCD methods of re-wrapping lunch meat on my grandfather's meticulous, waste-hating, near origami-perfect Saran method. I loved him.

Olivia, we do not choose our circumstances, the prejudices that we inherit, or our privilege or lack of it. It is my hope that for all the trouble and pain we have caused, it may be recognized that we are capable still of growth and amends. We are capable of expanding our table, our circle of love. It's on us to do it.

I hope I can make a sandwich for you some day. I am glad you are part of my family.

Auntie Phoebe here. Thanks so much, John, for pinch-hitting for me. Totes preesh. Also, I'm still reeling from that trip you and Wyatt took for your private mayonnaise label. That is a sentence I never thought I would write. Anyway, you are a scholar, a gentleman, and a saint, and I'm looking forward to Olivia coming to New York so she can take you up on that sandwich offer! OK, Livvie, I hope you enjoyed this crash-course in whiteness, and if you didn't, it's not my fault. Blame the white man. I've been doing that for years, and it only works like 6.3 percent of the time. But I'll take it!

Love,
Auntie Phoebe

Letter #5: Use Your Vagina Powers for Good

Dear Olivia,

If you are reading this solo, you're officially at the age where you're discovering your sexuality, yet you're probably uncomfortable when a grown-up like me uses the word *vagina*. I bet me writing the word *vagina* makes you want to roll your eyes so hard that they fall out your head and tumble into Lake Erie. And, to me, that is crazy! You'd rather be blind than see me use the word *vagina*? Coincidentally, some straight dudes would rather be blind than look at and go down on one. (If you're not reading this solo, my apologies to your mom and dad, but I can't sugarcoat the truth!) Anyway, the point is you might be grossed out by this whole vagina/vajayjay/vajeen talk, but we have to get into it because what you have going on down there is super powerful. And not because you can get pregnant and bring life into this world. Although creating a baby is pretty slick, your vajeen can do tons of other superhero things (refer back to "Dear Future Female President" essay and the whole "vagina changing color" thing), so you have to be mindful of what you're walking around with.

Being a woman is a very lucky and special thing, and normally, I'd pull a *People's Court* and present printouts and scanned documents pleading my case as to why you must use your vagina powers for good and not evil like breaking hearts or ensnaring world leaders in affairs that lead to war like—spoiler alert—Olivia Pope did in season four of *Scandie*. But that would end up being as long as this book, so I'm going to boil it down to one example of why you have to use your vagina powers for good and not waste it on BS, and that example is cribbed straight from the 2014 movie *Kingsman: The Secret Service*, starring my boo Colin Firth. Basically, I adore Colin because he always plays sensitive-ass dudes who would probably follow their ladies around 24/7 with a heating pad and go, "You OK, babe? You cramping, babe? You want some Häagen-Dazs, babe?" This may seem super lame to you right now because you're a young'un, but as you start to get older, you really appreciate the little things like your bae having Midol on standby. Anyway, Colin Firth is a cutie and despite not knowing much about the movie *Kingsmen*, I was down to watch it.

In it, Firth plays a fancy-pants spy named Harry Hart who trains Eggsy, a young bloke from the wrong side of the tracks, to become a spy. Turns out that Eggsy's dad was *also* a spy who worked alongside Harry and sacrificed his life to save H Squared and so Harry feels indebted. Except for the crazy stunts, violence, and double-crossing, the movie is mad chill until it nears the end. A bunch of leaders and dignitaries are being held captive because they didn't want to go along with Valentine's (Samuel L. Jackson) evil plan of committing mass genocide. One of these prisoners is the princess Tilde of Sweden (Hanna Alström), who gave us shades of badassness earlier in the film when she called out Valentine for his terrible scheme and refused to be bribed. Even though her prison conditions clearly weren't that bad because her makeup and hair are as flawless as Elsa's in *Frozen*, she cries out for Eggsy to save her once he arrives. His response? "Will you kiss me if I do?" *Oh. Hell. No* is what I'm thinking she's going to say. I'm planning on her going full #YesAllWomen with an epic speech that is going to culminate in her doing the lady version of a mic drop—dropping a container of Yaz birth control pills—and telling him she would rather rot in that cell than feel like she "owed" him affection in exchange for saving her life.

Olivia, that is not what she did. Instead, she goes (and I swear to you on my stack of Phylicia Rashad *Ebony* magazine covers that Tilde says this): "If you save the world, we can do it in the asshole." First of all, that is the weirdest way to let someone know you went to Catholic school. More important, how bad at negotiating is she that she reached the point in her young life where butt sex is *the go-to* bargaining chip? But that's not even the strangest part, Liv.

The worst part is the ending. Eggsy has saved the day and returns to her cell with a bottle of Champs. What does she do? Does she go, "J/K about that," the way my book club does when we all say we're going to read a self-help book for our next meeting, but then none of us do because television? No, she does not. Princess Tilde lies down on a grimy mattress and positions her butt immediately like anal is the *first* thing they're going to do. What the what? Even in a game of Double Dutch, people rock their bodies back and forth a few times to get into the rhythm of the swinging ropes before jumping in. This is insane, Olivia, and you are correct in assuming that after watching this scene, I logged onto GoDaddy.com and bought the website JesusBeAWigBecauseIm AboutToSnatchWhoeverWroteThisMovies Wig.org. Livvie, remember the following: Butt sex is not an amuse-bouche. Sure, sex is fun, but there is an order to it. You *gradually* progress. You don't start at the end with anal, then jump to the beginning with some fore-play, and then close on the middle like this is a Quentin Tarantino movie.

And I'm sorry, but out of everything—the blatant misogyny, the unrealistic sex propo-sition, the lack of attention to detail with the lube—what truly strains credibility here is that a grown woman of high status would willingly do it on a prison mattress that lacks any sort of lumbar support. Livvie, it may seem like I'm probably not picking my battles correctly, but I beg to differ. As a woman in her early thirties, my absolute bare minimum for hooking up with a dude is as follows: 1. He must have a job/be good-looking, 2. must treat me with respect, and 3. must have memory foam if he wants the dome. I hope that you use these criteria in your own life and start implementing them a decade earlier than I did.

OK, now that's all cleared up, let's get to why I singled out such an over-the-top example to prove a point. The point is that offering up sex to get a dude to do a thing he should already want to do is not using your vagina powers for good. That's the result of the patriarchy spending all of their time, energy, and money telling you that your worth lies between your legs (or in the case of *Kingsman,* your backside). So when I ask you to use your vagina powers for good, I mean when you achieve success, help keep the door open for the next class of women. Take pride in everything that makes you a woman and be an example that helps normalize the presence of women in male-dominated arenas. Use the insight that you have gained as a biracial woman and apply this knowledge to invent something, change an art form, break down barriers in the fields of math and science, or simply to better the lives of those around you. Just, please, for the love of everything sacred, do not waste your goodies and your powers on anyone or anything unworthy.

Love,
Auntie Phoebe

Letter #6: You, Too, Can Do

Dear Olivia,

Hey. So, yeah. I can't end this book on butt stuff. Don't get me wrong. I *was* going to do it. I told myself, "I'm going to be different. *Edgy.* I'm going to be bold and own it. Yep, I wrote all these interesting things and then I'm ending it all on the booty." But, Olivia. My parents—your grandparents—are black. You know this, but it is important to say it. And let me just further say, on average, because I don't want to generalize even though I'm totally correct in generalizing here, black parents Do. Not. Play. That. Edgy. In. Front. Of. White. Folk. Shit. Or edgy in front of *any* folk shit for that matter. They are not Team Take-the-Summer-Off-after-College-and-Travel-the-World-and-Figure-Out-Money-Later. They are not Team You-Can-Live-at-Home-for-an-Undetermined-Amount-of-Time-While-You-Find-Yourself. They are not Team Just-Express-Yourself-and-I-Support-All-Your-Decisions-No-Matter-How-Dumb-They-Are. And most important, they are not Team You-Going-to-Have-My-Last-Name-and-End-Your-Book-on-Butt-Stuff-When-You-Know-Damn-Well-the-People-That-Are-Going-to-Read-Your-Book-Will-Forever-Look-at-Us-as-the-Parents-of-the-Girl-Who-Ends-Her-Book-with-Butt-Stuff. Octavia Velina Robinson and Phillip Martin Robinson Sr. do not play that. *At all*. Why? I have a theory.

Now, don't get too excited. It's not a theory

based on substantiated facts or data or a tried-and-true formula. This is a theory based on being a black person who has black parents and being a black person who has seen other black people with their black parents. Black parents, for the most part, do not have that warm fuzzy place inside of them that some white parents have. That "it's all a part of the journey" chill vibe is missing, and in its place is a sense of urgency. There's no time to figure it out, make crazy mistakes, and have a laugh, because they know the playing field is not level. They know that at some point in life, their children will learn and keep relearning this fact, so there is no room for lollygagging or navel-gazing. And because there is this push from a lot of black parents for excellence, I believe that, deep down, the ultimate goal for black parents is that their child will end up on a Black History Month stamp. Sure, hardly anyone sends snail mail anymore, but the BHM stamp has a rarefied air. Like being awarded with a Kennedy Center Honor, or getting a Cronut before the local bakery sells out of them. But more important, the Black History Month stamp is indisputable. Only those who really changed the game, who were the first to achieve XYZ in their field, get to be on a stamp. And because there are still so many firsts yet to achieve, getting on a stamp, as uncommon as it is, still seems achievable. Difficult, but achievable. And if one is able to conquer this Herculean task, it is not only going to bring their family pride, but it lets other black boys and girls know that it's possible, and most important, that efforts of all the black people that came before them were not in vain.

That's why, I think, black parents are so hard on their kids. It's not just about potential bragging rights. While that's nice, what truly matters is that we be the "yes" to the "no" their parents heard.

Hell, black parents want us to be the "yes" to the "no" *they* received. It's why when I was being a slacker in high school and would get Cs like my white brethren, my parents would act the way Brenda Baker did at the end of *Boyz n the Hood* after her son Ricky was shot in a drive-by. My C and a white classmate's C are not the same. This truth sucks, but it is a truth that we live. It's why, on some level, all black parents are J. K. Simmons in *Whiplash* keeping the tempo, and for Octavia and Phillip, me ending this book on butt stuff is not their tempo. I need to keep their tempo. I need to live up to the Robinson name and live up to all the black people who came before me.

And if you think this sounds like a lot of pressure, it is. But is it? I mean, is it *really*? Definitely not to the black people that came before me. They were dodging water hoses, whippings, and N-bombs. All I have to do is keep my parents' tempo because they did not walk miles to work—literally, they did walk miles to work—to put me through a private prep school that would set me on the path of success in life, just so I, Phoebe Lynn Robinson, their only daughter, could end a book with "Girl, don't do anal unless it's on a nice Sealy Posturepedic." And certainly every single black person who has ever died— Sojourner Truth, Nat King Cole, Solomon Northup, black dudes who died peacefully in their sleep, the lady who died because she injected concrete in her behind to make her donk more donk-alicious, all the black people who died first in horror movies—did not perish so I can be the black girl who ends her book with butt stuff. So here I am, not ending this book on butt stuff and thereby keeping the hope alive that I will end up on a Black History Month stamp. You're welcome, Mom and Dad.

So if I'm not going to chuck up the deuces on a booty note, then what are going to be my final words? Something inspirational would be pretty rad, right? Sure, but that's even more pressure than keeping my parents' tempo, so I think the best that I can do here is offer up my troof. Not truth, but *troof* because troof is truer than truth. Troof keeps it all the way real. Truth is "Yes, those pants do make your butt look big." Troof is "Those pants do not make your butt *look* big. Your butt *is* big, and that's fine because those pants will never feel as good on as cake does in your mouth." So, Livvie, here is my troof about something that I think may inspire you, but most important, it is not about you-know-what stuff, so at least my parents will be happy about that.

About four and a half years ago, I had an LA-based manager, who is now my ex-manager. Let's call her Karen because for some reason people just don't like folks named Karen. Not me. One of my closest friends in life is a Karen, and I love her. She's fantastic, but she'll be the first to admit that she's encountered quite a few garbage Karens. To the world, Karens are fruitcake-bringing, living-in-a-state-of-indignance, time-wasting people whose go-to phrase is *This is unacceptable* when a very minor customer service affront goes down. This generalization is probably unfair. So break the mold! Don't have a Karen bias. Be the change I want to see in the world, girl. Except when it comes to my former comedy manager named "Karen." Fuck. Her.

So Karen. Let me give you a little background on this woman. Remember when the movie *Garden State* came out and people were charmed by it? They were like, "Ooooh, Zach Braff's button-down shirt matches the wallpaper he's standing in front of! So artsy. And wow, Natalie Portman is wearing braided pigtails and even though she's soooooooo pretty, she makes ugly, goofy faces to show how much she's a free spirit. I mean, she can go from looking like a 10 to looking like a 9.378 *because she just don't give a damn!*" Then a shift happened, and everyone was like, "*Hol'up!* This movie is bullshit. All these people are annoying. I now own all these CDs by the Shins. Da. Fuq." Karen is basically the human equivalent of that, except if you fast-forwarded past all the adoration and got right to "I now own all these CDs by the Shins. Da. Fuq." Karen was kind of the worst, and I kind of knew this going into our relationship. Her client who suggested me to her kind of knew this, but, as you'll see, when you're in your twenties, you spend so much time fighting against your correct instincts because you want to believe in the good of people. Although, if I'm being completely honest, I continued working with her even after getting wind of her suckage because she was the first manager I ever had, and I assumed that she was too good for me. Being a newbie in comedy is basically like an endless loop of Bambi learning how to walk on the ice pond, but instead of being charming while stumbling, we are desperate, eager, and operating on a combo of fear of being a fraud (read: not funny) and $1 pizza slices (because we're poor). So the fact that Karen seemed somewhat into me made me believe that she was my sole shot toward having a career. I didn't want to blow it. I wanted it so bad that I was afraid to lose something I didn't even have yet.

After I had been working with Karen for two months, she gave me glimpses of her suckage. She'd make plans, then break them last minute. She'd say she was coming to see my stand-up and then not show. Knowing that I was juggling a day job and stand-up at night, she once made a lunch date with me, and when I called her after twenty-five minutes of waiting, she told me she forgot and asked me if I would wait for her. "Uh, no, heaux. I can't just be gone for two hours from the job that gives me health benefits because you don't know how to input appointments in your Google calendar. I'm ordering this Swiss chard to go. Robinson out." I didn't say that. I wish I did. I just mumbled something about how it's "totally OK" that she forgot about her client and normally I'd wait another thirty minutes for her to get to me, but I had to get back to work. I hope she understood. *I* hope *she* understood. Olivia, what she did was classic "s/he just ain't that into you" behavior, but I mislabeled it "Manic Pixie Dream Girl" behavior à la the Portster in *Garden State* because Karen was quirky in the way that she legit wore her short bob in pigtails with elastic hair ties. Beware the pigtails. They will make you overlook things you shouldn't.

A few months later, I started a blog called Blaria (aka Black Daria) after I had written a short op-ed for *The New York Times* and remembered how much fun I had as a writer. After all, I went to school for writing, but sometimes life happens, and you get taken down other paths than the one you dream of in college. Those five hundred words in the *NYT*, where I got to be funny and smart, renewed my passion for writing and, more specifically, my passion for expressing my opinions uninterrupted by a pesky thing called people. That fire was enough for me to start Blaria. The happiness and warmth that coursed through my body when I was writing it sustained me, and after a few posts, a feeling settled over me. A little voice whispered in my ear, *You going to get a book deal out of this.* And from that moment, I was dead certain that it was going to happen. I had no idea how I had that much confidence in it. It was just a gut feeling, an instinct like how when I heard "Uptown Funk" for the first time, I started rocking along to the beat like I'd heard it at a thousand Chuck E. Cheese birthday parties. I knew that if I did the work, something good would come of this blog.

Twelve blog posts later, I had a phone call with Karen to catch her up on what I'd been doing. I was excited. The blog felt like the perfect marriage of my comedy chops I was honing from doing stand-up and my writing skills from my college days. Writing it made me feel alive. More than alive—I felt I had, at last, found my *purpose*. This blog, sharing unique social commentary and jokes about race, felt so natural to me that it was surprising. It was like I had found my home, a place where all my thoughts (some of which I didn't even realize I had within me until I had started typing) could live and be shared with other people who may feel similarly but didn't have the means to express themselves. This blog was what I had been envisioning my whole life. This blog was and is my American dream. Fuck a house, car, picket fence. Blaria was it. And I wanted to share the good news with Karen.

"So I started this blog," I said excitedly.

She responded with an "I saw..." that dangled in the air like a Cirque du Soleil dancer.

I was undeterred by her lack of enthusiasm. "I don't know. I'm just having fun, and I'm not sure how this will be a thing... but I just have a feeling that I could get a book deal out of this."

Without missing a beat, she responded, "Well, you aren't famous, so... maybe you should be doing something else." And then she carried on with the business she wanted to talk about, completely unaware that on my side of the phone, I felt like someone just pulled a Zack Morris "Time-out!" and rendered me frozen. I felt dumb. Embarrassed. *All my friends seemed excited about my blog. Were they just lying? Is she right? Is it already predestined that no one would be interested in a book written by me?* These thoughts flooded my brain as she went on about everything I should be doing instead of the blog. I don't remember much else from that phone call, but I do remember what happened when we hung up.

No, I thought to myself. "No," I *said* to myself as I stood in the living room of a friend's house where I was staying. No. What she said was bullshit. She *is* bullshit. I don't have to be famous to write a book. My friends weren't lying to me. And how dare she, as a white person, come take a dump on my hopes and then carry on with her day as if nothing just happened? Now, to be clear, I am quite aware that she might've had the same reaction if a non-black client of hers had a blog. I'll never know, but what I do know is this dismissiveness felt all too familiar to me as a woman and as a black person. The assumption was that I couldn't do it, which is something I have had to combat my whole life, and when the deliverer of this message is a white person, it knocks the wind out of me.

Yes, there are doubters of all shapes and sizes and races and sexual orientations, but given the history of this country, when a white person tells a person of color not to try something and to just stay on the bench, it really, deeply hurts. It feels like they know something you don't, some Wall Street insider-trading information on your life that reads:

LOL. YOUR DREAMS ARE BULLSHIT. THEY ARE QUIXOTIC. HOW UTTERLY SILLY OF YOU TO DREAM THE WAY YOU DO. JUST STOP, TAKE YOUR BALL, AND GO HOME.

At that moment, I knew we were done. I didn't fire her; our working partnership fizzled out a few weeks later because she didn't think I was viable enough as a client. But before the breakup? I was still naïve enough to think that it's OK to work with someone who has the balls to tell you flat-out that they don't believe in you. I tried to make it work and attempted to overlook the troof that it was killing me on the inside that yet another person—yet another white person in this comedy business—was telling me

I wasn't good enough. Add it to the pile of other things they have told me: that I'm too black, not black enough, not pretty enough, not sassy enough, can't handle pressure, not sure that I can bring it when it counts, that I'm too... me. "You know. Just a lot of... you." I think what you mean, sir, is that I'm a black lady. A blackity black black lady, with no diet version of me available. You have to take my high-calorie black ass or not at all.

Well, look at me now, Karen! I'm talking shit about you in a letter to my niece that is published in a book that you never thought my non-famous ass would get the chance to write. Sorry, Olivia. It is crass to gloat, but I just couldn't resist.

But this story isn't really about her. She's just the vessel that I'm using to make my point, which is this: Olivia, you are a Robinson. You are half-black. You are female. The deck is stacked against you. There will be far more people who don't believe in you than there will be who do simply because you're #TeamXX with non-white skin. There will be plenty of people who will write you off, ignore you, discount you, attempt to break you, and make it incredibly diffi-cult for you to achieve your goals. Tell you that you can't. Well, you can, despite the onslaught of negativity that will come your way telling you otherwise. Because there's one thing those negative forces didn't count on: Phillip Martin Robinson Jr. and Elizabeth Cristina Robinson raising you to be damn near impervious to negativity. So when you encounter your Karen, which you inevitably will, remember that your mom and dad raised you to keep their tempo, which is my parents', your grandparents', tempo, which is the tempo of the black people who came before them. Please, please, please keep their tempo, get yourself on a Black History Month stamp, and make Lisa Bonet proud.

Love always,
Auntie Phoebe

Acknowledgements

I know! When will this book end? Momentarily, I promise. I just have to give some shout-outs to the people I love and like very strongly. *Uh, I don't know you like that, Pheebs, so I'm not going to get a shout-out, am I?* Sorry. You won't, but I'm about to make it worth your while to stick around while I write nice things to other people OK. I *was* going to make it worth your while by including a photo of the cast of *Magic Mike XXL*, but then I realized I would have to pay to have a photo of all those hot dudes licensed for this book and that's ignorant.

I have already spent too much money on this movie—I saw it twice in theaters and rented it off iTunes to watch it at home—so if I spent any more money on *MMXXL*, I'm pretty sure Suze Orman would magically appear and body-slam me for making poor financial decisions. But, please, dear reader, don't mistake my cheapness as a sign of my lack of devotion to *XXL*. I, in all sincerity, believe that the film is the answer to the question Judy Blume posed forty-six years ago: "Are you there God? It's me, Margaret." God was like, "Sorry for

319

being late, boo. I gotchu," and then winked and blessed Marg and everyone else's eyeballs and libidos with *Magic Mike XXL*. And yes, God, in this scenario is Stanley Tucci's character from *The Devil Wears Prada* dipped in chocolate. Anyway, the picture is not in the book, but thanks to Googs, we can all take a few moments to take in the greatness that is Channing Tatum, Matt Bomer, Joe Manganiello, Adam Rodriguez, and for the older peeps, Kevin Nash. *Whoo! Mmm!* Aaaaaaaaaaaand, we're back! Now onward with the thank-yous.

First, to my amazing parents, Phil and Octavia, thank you for everything. I am so lucky that you're my mom and dad. You made me fearless, smart, funny, and a good citizen of this planet, and you give the best advice and tough love when I need it the most, and you laugh at all my jokes. You also annoy me because you're right about most things. Let me be right about some of the things. OK, one thing. Anything, I beg of you. I love you.

Thanks to PJ (Phil Jr.) and Liz or "Phiz and Lil," as you were affectionately called in college. You remind me to not be such a workaholic because I'm always on the verge of living that Katherine Heigl in *27 Dresses* life. You're also always very excited for everything I accomplish, no matter how small it is, and your enthusiasm is so touching. You guys are very busy and you make time for me and for yourselves. I want to be you when I grow up.

Olivia, at the writing of this, you had recently gone

potty by yourself for the first time and when my dad/ your granddad sent me a picture of your boo-boo in the toilet, I went, "Aww, that is the cutest thing." You have clearly opened my heart bigger than I ever imagined. Thanks for that.

Thanks to Robert Guinsler for reading a list about funny NYC comedians last year and then shooting me an e-mail with a query, "Do you want to write a book?" That was the e-mail I had been hoping to get for three years. You are a delight. I love talking about boys and Viola Davis with you. And quite frankly, those are the only two things anyone ever needs to talk about.

Thank you, thank you, thank you to Kate Napolitano, my lovely and badass editor, who is younger than me, has a better phone voice than me, and is a natural redhead (I get my red hair from Vivica A. Fox's hair line). We began this journey with me saying to you, "I've only blogged. I need your help because I've never written a book before. I don't know what I'm doing." And you have been there every step of the way, offering guidance, putting up with me missing practically every deadline along the way because I work about seven jobs at all times (LOL/ UGH), cheering me up, and pushing me to deliver the book that we both knew I had in me. I wouldn't want anyone else by my side. Can't wait to do this again with you.

Chenoa, my manager. I can be moody. I can be flighty. I can be overwhelmed. I can be on top of the world. I can and do send you e-mails at 2 a.m. because I'm constantly working. And you put up with all of it. Thank you. You are amazing. I tell you that all the time, so at least I'm grateful, but I want to tell you again here.

Thanks to Jessica. You are my work wife. You are my sister from another mister. Thank you for coming into my life and making this stand-up comic—who can, like all comics, resist having a creative partner because I like to control everything—be open to one of the best relationships of my life. I love you. And I will keep harassing you about that "bloop bloop."

Thanks to Joanna Solotaroff, Jen Poyant, Paula Schuzman (aka *Felicity*, season one), Dean Cappello, Daisy Rosario, Rachel Neel (thanks for sharing my love of Bono, boo!), Laura Walker, Delaney Simmons, and everyone at WNYC for being the home of the *2 Dope Queens* and *Sooo Many White Guys* podcasts. You totally and completely get what Jess and I are doing, and you give us free rein to make the art that we wanna make. The amount of trust and faith you have in two black ladies in comedy, as well as your letting me branch off solo for *SMWG*, does not go unnoticed. Neither does your allowing me to be wildly inappropriate in business meetings.

Thanks to John Hodgman for writing a guest letter. I know how busy you are. You are so kind.

Thanks to Mindy Tucker for the kick-ass cover photo and all the pictures of me you have taken over the years.

You are a genius and so beloved by everyone you meet. Keep shining, boo!

Thanks to my comedy family and real-life friends: Jamie Lee (I mean…), Baron Vaughn, Ilana Glazer (I love you so much. #YASQUEEN!), Michelle Buteau, Naomi Ekperigin, Rae Sanni, Maeve Higgins, Josh Ruben, David Lee Nelson, Amy Aniobi, Julie Miller, Anu Valia, Nore Davis, Franchesca Ramsey, Kelly Anneken, Chris Lamberth, Merrill Davis, Rose Surnow (Mess Hall is legit the best place ever), *White Guy Talk Show* crew (we have kept our text message chain going for two years. We are incredible), Marianne Ways for always throwing me up on a show when I need the stage time, Wyatt Cenac, and Beth McGregor (you live all the way in London, so we don't get to see each other, but you are so sweet to me, and I cherish the e-mails you send me).

Thanks to real-life friends who don't do comedy: Alison Stauver (we live in the butthole of Brooklyn, mere avenues away from each other. Thanks for being my plus-one in life), Karen Asprea (you're one of my oldest friends. I love you), the Picturehouse Crew (we don't see each other nearly enough, but I love you all), Mark McCreary, Josh Sussman (I was an OK admin assistant for you, and you didn't care because you supported me doing stand-up from the day I met you and also Katya rocks! Hey, boo!), and Safy Farah (we have been Internet friends for so long, and it was so wonderful to finally meet you this year; I am envious of your teeth). Thanks to everyone who has read one of my Blaria blogs, my rants on Facebook, and/or attended any of my stand-up shows. I would not be here without you.

Finally, Michael Fassbender, thanks in advance for being my future baby daddy.

About the Author

Phoebe Robinson is a stand-up comedian, writer, and actress whom Vulture.com, Essence, and Esquire have named one of the top comedians to watch. She has appeared on NBC's Late Night with Seth Meyers and Last Call with Carson Daly; Comedy Central's Broad City, The Nightly Show with Larry Wilmore, and @ midnight with Chris Hardwick; as well as Amazon's I Love Dick. Robinson's writing has been featured in The Village Voice and on Glamour.com, TheDailyBeast.com, VanityFair.com, Vulture.com, and NYTimes.com. She was also a staff writer on MTV's hit talking head show, Girl Code, as well as a consultant on season three of Broad City. Most recently, she created and starred in Refinery29's web series Woke Bae, and alongside Jessica Williams of The Daily Show, she is the creator and co-star of the hit WNYC podcast 2 Dope Queens as well as the creator and host of the new WNYC podcast Sooo Many White Guys. Robinson lives and performs stand-up in Brooklyn, New York, and you can read her weekly musings about race, gender, and pop culture on her blog, Blaria.com (aka Black Daria).